The Labrador Retriever

Katya Darlington

John Bartholomew & Son Limited
Edinburgh

*The Publisher wishes to thank The Kennel Club and The American
Kennel Club for permission to reproduce the breed standards.*

First published in Great Britain 1977 *by*
JOHN BARTHOLOMEW & SON LIMITED
12 Duncan Street, Edinburgh EH9 1TA

ISBN 0 7028 1094 0

1st edition

Reprinted 1982, 1985

Prepared for the Publisher by Youé & Spooner Ltd.
Colour illustrations by Charles Rush; airbrush drawings by Malcolm Ward

Printed in Great Britain by John Bartholomew & Son Limited

Contents

Preface

As a working gundog the merits of the Labrador have been recognised for more than a century. As workers for the Guide Dogs for the Blind, the breed has long been one of the mainstays. As companions they are now amongst the top dogs. This book has been written for the companion dog owner and describes fully the pleasures and the pitfalls of owning so intelligent, kindly and active an animal. Everything a novice pet owner needs to know is here. The author is one of the best known of Labrador breeders and judges and in these pages she shares a lifetime's experience. Emphasis is placed throughout on responsible ownership, for the pet dog needs to be a disciplined, sociable animal confident and secure in its role as a loyal and affectionate companion.

Wendy Boorer
Consultant Editor

Introduction

This book is written almost entirely for the owners of pet Labradors from puppyhood onwards. I have tried to go back to my own start in the breed so many years ago, and have mentioned the difficulties and questions that I myself remember coming up against. I have also tried to be careful to avoid any technical terms, and if I have had to use them I have tried to explain them.

I would always advise you to think carefully before embarking on being a Labrador owner. Labradors are the best of pets and companions if managed correctly but can become menaces, as they grow big, if they are not properly looked after and controlled.

So when you eventually, after much thought, decide to buy a Labrador, make up your mind to be a really good, conscientious, sensible owner and you will have a good, obedient, trouble-free dog. But be lax in any way and you and your dog will be the worst citizens in your neighbourhood, dreaded by all.

I have tried so hard to help you; please reward me by having a nice, kind, well-behaved Labrador, so that you and your dog are a credit to the breed, and an example to those careless owners of disobedient, dangerous pets of any breed.

Breed history

The most important thing that you have to decide before going off to purchase your first Labrador is whether you really want one, and to do this it is a help to know something of the history, for this explains the whys and wherefores of a Labrador and why it is like it is.

The Labrador was a fisherman's water dog found, in the early 1800s, in the seaports of Newfoundland (funnily enough not in Labrador, and why it has that name we can only guess). It was seen by various travellers, hanging about the waterfronts of the fishing ports of that barren coast, boarding any ship it fancied, often sailing with the cod boats to England, where there was a trade with Poole Harbour in Dorset, and jumping ship there to hang about the English quaysides until another boat it fancied arrived to carry it back to St. John's, Newfoundland. Incidentally, the St. John's Newfoundland was its earlier name.

In this way the Labrador gradually appeared in England and, as it was a utility dog with strong retrieving instincts, especially from water, it soon became incorporated into a few of the shooting kennels of the sporting English landowners, who found it excellent for collecting wounded game, both from water and on land.

From about 1875 it gradually grew in numbers and popularity until today it is one of the most popular and numerous breeds in Britain and indeed is spreading all over the world.

Before you decide to go out and buy that appealing little puppy, it is as well to remember that the Labrador is by nature a medium to biggish dog when fully grown, of sporting instincts with a great fondness for mud and water in which it loves to slosh about whenever it gets the slightest chance. When a youngster the dog has an abundance of energy going spare, unless its exuberance and need to use its mouth for retrieving something is turned into useful channels.

For a family it is ideal, because the Labradors, when on the cod boats of Newfoundland, went with any ship, sat in with any crew, or lived *en famille* especially in the bitter winters. Indeed it was everyone's dog and everyone's friend and helper, and still retains this cheerful, obliging character to this day.

7

Points of the Labrador

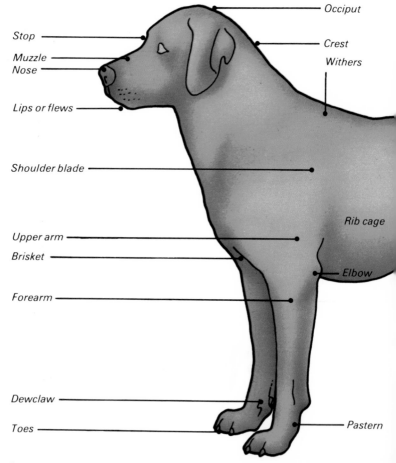

Occiput

Stop

Crest

Muzzle

Withers

Nose

Lips or flews

Shoulder blade

Rib cage

Upper arm

Brisket

Elbow

Forearm

Dewclaw

Toes

Pastern

8

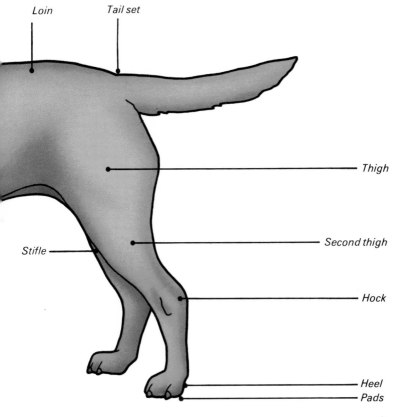

Loin

Tail set

Thigh

Second thigh

Stifle

Hock

Heel

Pads

9

For this reason, and also because it has a short, very easy and naturally clean coat, it is a firm family favourite and one of the most common and popular house and family dogs to be found anywhere.

But before buying your first puppy, do just think and think hard. It will grow. Are you prepared for a biggish dog? It will eat. Can you afford to give it the good food, including meat, that it will need? It will need a place to sleep, a place to exercise, a place where it can be shut out of harm's way if you have to leave it for an hour or two. Can you give it those necessities? Have you room and time?

If you can resolve these problems satisfactorily, then go ahead and buy a puppy from a reputable source (and I stress that word 'reputable'), but always remember that those early Labradors on the cod banks of Newfoundland were essentially working and water dogs, with a need for exercise, food, a job in life and a bit of care and attention to enable them to become the happy, healthy, family dog that you are hoping for. A lot will depend on you.

A good retrieve of a woodcock, showing speed, style and willingness to return to its owner as soon as possible

The breed standard

The British Breed Standard

General Appearance *The general appearance of the Labrador should be that of a strongly-built, short-coupled, very active dog, broad in the skull, broad and deep through the chest and ribs, broad and strong over the loins and hindquarters. The coat close, short with dense undercoat and free from feather. The dog must move neither too wide nor too close in front or behind, he must stand and move true all round on legs and feet.*

Head and Skull *The skull should be broad with a pronounced stop so that the skull is not in a straight line with the nose. The head should be clean cut without fleshy cheeks. The jaws should be medium length and powerful and free from snipiness. The nose wide and the nostrils well developed.*

Eyes *The eyes, of medium size expressing intelligence and good temper, should be brown or hazel.*

Ears *Should not be large and heavy and should hang close to the head, and set rather far back.*

Mouth *Teeth should be sound and strong. The lower teeth just behind but touching the upper.*

Neck *Should be clean, strong and powerful and set into well placed shoulders.*

Forequarters *The shoulders should be long and sloping. The forelegs well boned and straight from the shoulder to the ground when viewed from either the front or side. The dog must move neither too wide nor too close in front.*

Body *The chest must be of good width and depth with well-sprung ribs. The back should be short coupled.*

Hindquarters *The loins must be wide and strong with well-turned stifles; hindquarters well developed and not sloping to the tail. The hocks should be slightly bent and the dog must neither be cow-hocked nor move too wide or too close behind.*

Feet *Should be round and compact with well-arched toes and well-developed pads.*

Tail *The tail is a distinctive feature of the breed; it should be very thick towards the base, gradually tapering towards the tip, of medium length and practically free from any feathering, but clothed thickly all round with the Labrador's short, thick, dense coat, thus giving that peculiar 'rounded' appearance*

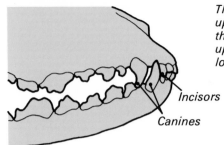

The correct 'scissors bite'. The upper incisors fit closely over the lower incisors and the upper canines fit behind the lower canines.

Incisors

Canines

which has been described as the 'Otter' tail. The tail may be carried gaily, but should not curl over the back.

Coat *The coat is another distinctive feature of the breed, it should be short and dense and without wave with a weather-resisting undercoat and should give a fairly hard feeling to the hand.*

Colour *The colour is generally black or yellow – but other whole colours are permitted. The coat should be free from any white markings but a small white spot on the chest is allowable. The coat should be of a whole colour and not of a flecked appearance.*

Weight and Size *Desired height for Dogs, 22-22½in. (55.9-57.2cm.); Bitches, 21½-22in. (54.6-55.9cm.).*

Faults *Under or overshot mouth; no undercoat; bad action; feathering; snipiness on the head; large or heavy ears; cow-hocked; tail curled over back.*

Note *Male animals should have two apparently normal testicles fully descended into the scrotum.*

The American Breed Standard

General Appearance *The general appearance of the Labrador should be that of a strongly built, short-coupled, very active dog. He should be fairly wide over the loins, and strong and muscular in the hindquarters. The coat should be close, short, dense and free from feather.*

Head *The skull should be wide, giving brain room; there should be a slight stop, i.e. the brow should be slightly pronounced, so that the skull is not absolutely in a straight line with the nose. The head should be clean-cut and free from fleshy cheeks. The jaws should be long and powerful and free*

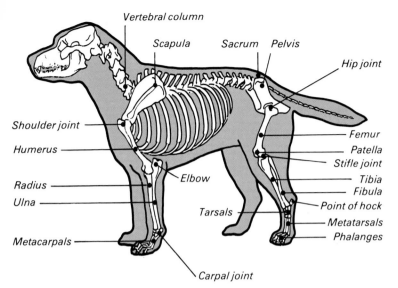

Vertebral column
Scapula Sacrum Pelvis
Hip joint
Shoulder joint
Femur
Humerus
Patella
Stifle joint
Radius
Elbow
Tibia
Fibula
Ulna
Point of hock
Tarsals
Metatarsals
Phalanges
Metacarpals
Carpal joint

from snipiness; the nose should be wide and the nostrils well developed. Teeth should be strong and regular, with a level mouth. The ears should hang moderately close to the head, rather far back, should be set somewhat low and not be large and heavy. The eyes should be of a medium size, expressing great intelligence and good temper, and can be brown, yellow or black, but brown or black is preferred.

Neck and Chest The neck should be medium length, powerful and not throaty. The shoulders should be long and sloping. The chest must be of good width and depth, the ribs well sprung and the loins wide and strong, stifles well turned, and the hindquarters well developed and of great power.

Legs and Feet The legs must be straight from the shoulder to ground, and the feet compact with toes well arched, and pads well developed; the hocks should be well bent, and the dog must neither be cowhocked nor be too wide behind; in fact, he must stand and move true all round on legs and feet. Legs should be of medium length, showing good bone and muscle, but not so short as to be out of balance with rest of body. In fact, a dog well balanced in all points is preferable to one with outstanding good qualities and defects.

Tail The tail is a distinctive feature of the breed; it should be very thick towards the base, gradually tapering towards the

13

tip, of medium length, should be free from any feathering, and should be clothed thickly all round with the Labrador's short, thick, dense coat, thus giving that peculiar 'rounded' appearance which has been described as the 'otter' tail. The tail may be carried gaily but should not curl over the back.

Coat *The coat is another very distinctive feature; it should be short, very dense and without wave, and should give a fairly hard feeling to the hand.*

Color *The colors are black, yellow, or chocolate and are evaluated as follows:*

(a) Blacks: All black, with a small white spot on chest permissible. Eyes to be of medium size, expressing intelligence and good temper, preferably brown or hazel, although black or yellow is permissible.

(b) Yellows: Yellows may vary in colour from fox-red to light cream with variations in the shading of the coat on ears, the underparts of the dog, or beneath the tail. A small white spot on chest is permissible. Eye coloring and expression should be the same as that of the blacks, with black or dark brown eye rims. The nose should also be black or dark brown, although 'fading' to pink in winter weather is not serious. A 'Dudley' nose (pink without pigmentation), should be penalized.

(c) Chocolates: Shades ranging from light sedge to chocolate. A small white spot on chest is permissible. Eyes to be light brown to clear yellow. Nose and eye-rim pigmentation dark brown or liver colored. 'Fading' to pink in winter weather not serious. 'Dudley' nose should be penalized.

Movement *Movement should be free and effortless. The forelegs should be strong, straight and true, and correctly placed. Watching a dog move towards one, there should be no signs of elbows being out in front, but neatly held to the body with legs not too close together, but moving straight forward without pacing or weaving. Upon viewing the dog from the rear, one should get the impression that the hind legs, which should be well muscled and not cowhocked, move as nearly parallel as possible, with hocks doing their full share of work and flexing well, thus giving the appearance of power and strength.*

Approximate weights of dogs and bitches in working condition *Dogs 60-75lb. (27.21-34.01kg.); bitches 55-70lb. (24.95-31.78kg.).* **Height at Shoulders** *Dogs 22½-24½in. (57.2-62.2cm.); bitches 21½-23½in. (54.6-59.7cm.).*

The lovely yellow Labrador bitch
Sh. Ch. Sandylands Mercy

A splendid young chocolate dog
Lawnwoods Hot Chocolate

One of the best black Labradors in the UK
Sh. Ch. Sandylands Storm-Along

Choosing a puppy

I have already advised you to buy your Labrador from a reputable source, and I stress that generally speaking it is better to buy from a breeder than from a dealer. A reputable breeder will do his best to get you suited with a healthy puppy that you will like and that will be a good advertisement for his kennel name.

He is concerned for the welfare of his puppies and will try to make redress for anything that goes wrong which can be attributed to the breeder or kennel. Therefore, buy from a breeder, and a well-known one if possible, and pay the fair market price. A cut-price pup is never satisfactory, because there is a reason for the cut in price. Either the puppies have not been reared well enough, or there have been too many reared on the bitch so that the whole of the litter has been weakened in the struggle to survive, or the breeding is not good enough.

Your local pet store will often help you in your search for a good source for a puppy. They know the *good* Labrador breeders in the vicinity and, as it is to their advantage over the next few years when they will be supplying the puppy's food, they will want you to get a satisfactory one. If they themselves cannot put you on to a good breeder, they can at least tell you where your local canine club operates and the name of the secretary who will help you. Failing that, the pet shop will be able to look at one of the canine papers and give you a name and address from that.

'Buy from a breeder' is a good motto, and my very strong, and indeed only, advice is to stick to it.

Having found the name of a reputable breeder, make an appointment to visit the kennels. There you will be able to see the dogs and talk to the owner. Here I must point out that the label 'a reputable breeder' means he or she is considered reliable, so if you wish to get the best help, you must prove reliable too. Keep the appointment at the right time on the right day. In that way you start off on the right foot. You would be surprised how many do not turn up or bother to let the breeder know they are not coming.

Another hint worth passing on, from the breeder's point of view, is to treat the appointment as a business afternoon, not a trip out for the mother-in-law and old folks or babies. There is a sensible reason for this, which is that this is the only moment you have to pick the brains of that breeder, to make a lot of important decisions and to go into things thoroughly. If the old folks are in the car and getting chilled, or the baby is howling and the tiny children getting tired and bored, you will not make full use of your time, so go unencumbered as far as possible.

Personally, as a breeder trying to do the best for my clients, I like to see the husband and the wife and perhaps one or two children so that I can decide whether they *all* like the puppy and are the sort of people to have one. (Yes, we like to 'vet' you, just as you like to weigh us up and our dogs.)

A typical yellow puppy

Before buying your pup there are four things to consider:

1. Whether you have time, money, kennel space, and enough exercising space for a puppy.
2. Whether you *all,* especially the wife, want a puppy, remembering that on the wife falls the work of looking after it.
3. Whether you can afford to feed what will be a big dog.
4. Whether you have enough money to pay for the puppy.

These things would seem too obvious to mention, but unfortunately the idea of having a puppy often stems from seeing an attractive specimen of the breed on the television, or possibly thinking it would be a nice Christmas present for the children and going off and buying one, without giving it any other thought at all.

Personally, I like my clients to come and see their puppy at about four or five weeks old and to ask me all about the pup's food, bed, collar and lead, etc. Then they can go home and arrange these all-important things and come again and collect the puppy at about eight weeks, with all the plans made and everything ready for it. If we see a nice married couple like the puppy, and two or three well-ordered, well-disciplined and sensible children, then we feel the puppy itself has a hope of being a good citizen, being properly looked after, loved and disciplined kindly and firmly.

If you are buying just for a pet, it is usual and satisfactory to buy the puppy and take delivery of it at about eight weeks. By this time the puppy should have been properly wormed, flea-powdered, its nails cut and its weaning from its mother carried out correctly so that it is on real food and able to leave its litter mates and sleep by itself without harm. You will probably find that the breeder has chosen one or two puppies for himself and perhaps allotted one or two for overseas, but that there are still one, two, or three for you to choose from.

I cannot guide your choice except to say: *do not* pick a shy and nervous one; *do not* pick one that growls or snaps; *do not* pick one with runny nose and eyes, or any sign of skin trouble; *do not* pick the little runt because you feel that you must save it from a hard time and give it love and care.

I will not say *do not* pick the biggest, because that depends on your circumstances, but I advise you to think twice before going for the biggest and therefore to you by far the best puppy. It may look as though it is going to be the champion of them all, just because it is big and handsome, but in a breed like the Labrador the best is usually the normal-sized one and very seldom the grand big one, which becomes overdone, i.e. rather gross and ponderous, with age and maturity. You also have to consider whether you want to end up with a huge dog in today's circumstances, when the middle-sized pup of the litter is going to grow as big as his parents or thereabouts, and the huge puppy may be outsize when fully grown.

My advice is to go for a nice, happy, cheerful pup of medium size with nice nut-brown eyes, a good coat, a broad head and muzzle, medium-sized ears, broad, short body, short, thick tail and *medium*-sized feet. Although the layman seems to think that huge, floppy feet and huge, floppy ears are something very desirable, they are *not* correct in a Labrador, which when grown should have small ears and compact feet.

Make sure the puppy has been wormed, and ask when you must do this again. Find out when you must inoculate it against the dreaded diseases distemper, hardpad and the jaundice type illnesses. Ask if the nails have been attended to and make sure that all the puppy's papers are in order.

This is very important nowadays because the Kennel Club has become very strict in recent years and if you are paying for a pedigree puppy with all the good things that implies, then you must make sure the papers are in order. Then if you ever want to, and the dog turns out well, you can reap a little benefit and possibly a small money-harvest in return for your outlay, cost of feeding, etc., and all your love and care. If the papers are not in order, then you may never be able to remedy this under the new regulations of 'closing the books' at the Kennel Club. These state that only puppies from properly registered stock can in their turn be registered. So make absolutely sure the papers are in order, or the puppy's value is gone.

Before you take your puppy home, ask the breeder about its food, making sure you know what it must have to eat, how many meals, etc., and when. The breeder will start you off right over this, but he can tell you only the approximate amounts and the right types of food for the present. The future is up to you. The great thing is to get the puppy safely over the change of home and get it eating well and without tummy upsets; from there you gradually increase its food while decreasing the number of feeds per day, and varying the type of food until it is off puppy food and on to an adult diet of (eventually) one good square meal a day.

Be warned and listen to the breeder carefully when he describes the food. Get it written down, and then follow it until the puppy progresses beyond it. What I am trying to say is that if the breeder says, 'Give raw meat,' then give raw meat. Soya protein will not do. By meat we mean red meat, by tripe we mean tripe and not heart, and so on. If we say 'heart' we mean it, and liver is not the same as lights. Real red meat is necessary for a growing puppy; fish, poultry, rabbit, liver and the various offals such as tripe are excellent as well, but do not replace meat.

A Labrador is going to put on a great amount of substance and bone during its growth, more in proportion to its medium-sized body than nearly any other breed, being a stocky, sturdy fellow for its size. It needs real body-rearing foods to do this, just as a human boxer does, and good food *must* go into the dog between eight weeks and eight months.

Ask your breeder about the diet and then carry it out to the best of your ability, and the dog should thrive and its health give you very little trouble.

The breeder will tell you when the puppy is old enough to leave the mother and its litter mates, but a word of warning here. You may find it inconvenient to collect the puppy the week the breeder tells you is the best and so may try and persuade the breeder to let you have it a week earlier. A puppy should *not,* and I repeat *not,* leave the nest until it is at least seven and a half or eight weeks old. To take it earlier than this is asking for trouble and the puppy will go back in condition instead of progressing. It *must* be that age at least and preferably over eight weeks old. That is the optimum time for it to leave and you will be wise to stick to this. It is better a week later than a week earlier, but even then there are certain difficulties in timing the injections, etc., so it is better to stick exactly to the eight weeks rule.

General care for a puppy

Make sure you have everything ready at home before you go to collect the pup, having consulted the breeder about the correct bed and where to put it, the right food (do not make any change at first), and that you have a food dish and water bowl and somewhere you can keep the puppy closely confined at first. It must be out of draughts, and the bed slightly raised off the floor, and the floor must not be chilly and cold, i.e. stone or concrete. When you have all these things ready, and the pup is seven and a half or eight weeks old, you can go to collect it. Take a supply of newspapers in case the puppy is sick in the car, and your cash in hand (although breeders accept cheques very often, it is asking a little much when dealing with a stranger, so I advise cash), get all your instructions and the puppy's papers and get it home trying to keep it from getting chilled on the journey.

If you intend to keep the puppy as a house dog, make sure it has a suitable raised bed in the place where you intend it to live, so that from the first it sleeps in its own bed and place. It is also wise to have a bed for it or at least a rug in every room, so that it lies there and not all over the place under everyone's feet.

When you arrive home with your new purchase, it will probably be towards evening. The children will want to have a little play with the new puppy, but remember it is still very young indeed, tires very quickly and will also be feeling strange without its mates to back it up. So after a little while give the pup its dinner just as you have been instructed by the breeder.

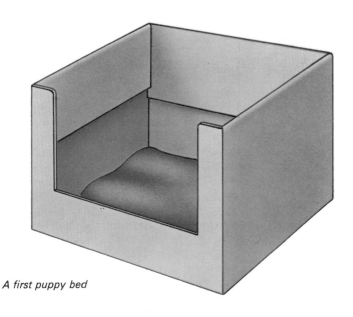

A first puppy bed

After its meal take it out for a little time on to the patch of grass you intend it to use for the future, and stand by until you see it has done what it should. The puppy will do this naturally after a meal so this is your chance to start its house training after its first meal in your house.

When the puppy has relieved itself and has had a little gambol on the grass, take it to its bed and make a firm rule that it is not disturbed by the children or curious visitors. The puppy needs its rest, and must be allowed to go into a deep sleep in its bed, snug and warm with a blanket against its back. Remember that it will badly miss the protection of the furry backs of its brothers and sisters snuggling up to it, so chills, especially to the back, must be avoided.

You will have provided the puppy with a high-sided box, perhaps a cardboard carton from the grocer for its first few nights, and will put the dog right into it so that it cannot get out to sleep on a cold floor with its back in a draught. Afterwards you must provide a proper, raised, draughtproof bed for it in a safe place. The puppy should have a blanket or woolly jumper in its bed to lie on.

After a cry or two because it is lonely, the puppy will drop off to sleep, provided it is snug enough. Then let sleeping dogs lie until towards your bedtime. When you are having your nightcap and getting your hot-water bottles ready, give the puppy a warming meal of baby cereal with milk (which is what I give last thing). This will warm its tummy, make it happy and sleepy again, give it some much needed comfort in its loneliness and will last it till morning.

First thing next morning the puppy must have an easily digested breakfast which it can eat quickly without harm, because it may be ravenous and tend to gobble. I give brown bread, any meat or chicken scraps from last night's dinner-plates and make it up in bulk with cornflakes and milk. I do *not* recommend porridge. I also often add a little well-soaked puppy meal. The puppy can have an egg on this meal and any supplement you are giving it, such as vitamin B tablets and calcium with vitamin D and the correct amount of phosphate which you can buy from any good chemist.

Immediately the dog has had its breakfast, take it out into the garden on to that same patch of grass, after which it must have a very good play to get rid of its surplus spirits and energy and to exercise its muscles and lungs. The puppy needs this free play badly and must have it. As soon as it starts to sit about, put it back to bed till noon.

At noon the puppy will be ready for its midday snack, which is when I give its daily raw meat, at this age buying raw mince from the butcher, paying for the best and leanest. At this age the puppy needs only about a golfball-sized dollop of raw meat and I give a little drink of milk as well to make it go down nicely. Then take it out to the garden for another good play.

Let it sleep till supper which is its main meal and should be of good size, full of good food, based on puppy meal soaked with broth in which vegetables have been cooked, with cooked meat chopped finely added. Fish, cheese, chicken, rabbit or any other meat protein goes on this meal. It must *not* be sloppy or the puppy's bowels will be loose. Keep the meal firm but crumbly. I do not give egg or milk at the evening meal, because the puppy has had this for breakfast and with its midday meat. Give it plenty without gorging it. I cannot give you any measure because every puppy differs, but if you look at the puppy's stomach, you can gauge it yourself, so that the dog is pleasantly full without being gorged. Take the puppy out to the garden to play again, and then back to bed till it is time for its bedtime feed.

This will be the routine for a few weeks to come. The only addition I have not mentioned is that all dogs must have clean, cold water handy *all the time.* The puppy may drink very little, some dogs do, especially in winter, but even if it never seems to drink, the water must still be there. A proper bowl is necessary because Labradors are water dogs born and bred and will upset their bowl if it is too light, emptying it and carrying it about in their mouths dripping over everything. So the bowl must be heavy; do not put too much in at a time. Make sure the bowl is not too shallow, otherwise the puppy will spend its time digging in it and making a fearful splashing and mess all over walls and floor. Buy a proper, steep-sided, rather heavy, purpose-made drinking bowl and then keep it clean and full at all times.

If on about the third day the puppy's digestion becomes a bit upset, which is very common and is due to a combination of change of water, change of air, slight change of diet, and possibly a feeling of chill at night, then cut out the milk altogether and make the food *stiffer.* Give stiff rice puddings made with only a little milk and mostly water, until the starchy

DIET SHEET FOR SMALL PUPPIES

	18th day onwards	24th day onwards	4–7 weeks	7 weeks onwards
BREAKFAST	Farex and milk. (Goat's milk is always preferable to cow's milk).	Brown bread well soaked in milk. Add coddled egg or finely scraped raw beef.	Puppy meal (No. 1 size) soaked with hot water-milk added. Finely chopped meat, fish, chicken, rabbit or coddled egg.	Good breakfast. Brown bread or No.2 biscuit soaked with hot water. Milk, meat, fish, egg, etc. ADD CALDECIUM (calcium and Vitamin D).
LUNCH	Bitch does the feeding as before	Raw mince and a little milk.	Raw mince and milk.	CUT OUT (add meat to evening meal instead).
SUPPER	ditto	As breakfast with scraped meat, finely chopped chicken or fish. (Coddled egg only once a day.)	A GOOD meal, as breakfast only bigger and with more meat, etc.	GOOD SUPPER. Soaked biscuit (No.2), meat, scraps, chicken, fish, etc. Vegetables.
LAST THING AT NIGHT	Farex and milk.	Farex and milk.	CUT OUT	—

USE YOUR COMMON SENSE – judge the size of each meal by the size of the puppy's tummy. Remember plenty of meat and other protein. Also vegetables when the puppy is older. As adult – 3 parts biscuit to 1 part meat. Scraps, vegetables, etc. extra. When adult, one meal a day, unless under stress.

rice puddings tighten its bowels up again. Then resume normal food gradually. Cows' milk and raw liver are both aperients for puppies and will give them diarrhoea, and indeed raw liver should never be given all the dog's life, being good only if well cooked, and in smallish quantities. Goats' milk is the best of all for puppies. If you can get it, it is worth the trouble.

The puppy's routine is eat, relieve itself, play, sleep, in that order, all through the day for the first week or so, and it should thrive on it.

Once the puppy is fully settled into its routine and it is digesting its food properly, you should start thinking about inoculations. The dog *must have* these. Ask your vet what injections he advises. He will certainly advise protection against distemper and hardpad, those twin deadly diseases; and possibly against the jaundice types of disease. The puppy can have these three vaccines combined, probably given in two stages, one a couple of weeks or so after the other. Your vet will tell you exactly when to bring the puppy, but *do not,*

Feeding utensils

whatever you do, take it to be done if it is the slightest bit off-colour. The puppy must be absolutely fit and well, tight in its motions and with no sign of runny eyes or tummy upset. Puppy owners, unless professional breeders, have a strong tendency to say, 'He's all right. He's only got a little cold, or chill,' or 'It's just something he ate.' Well, whatever it is, don't kid yourself into taking the chance. If the puppy is not absolutely healthy do not have it injected. As soon as it is fit, after it is about nine weeks old, *get it done.* This is a *must,* take it from me.

Keep the puppy quiet for a few days until it gets over the effects, because there will be a slight effect, even if it is not apparent. The puppy is really having and fighting a very slight dose of distemper and needs a little quiet to help it recover. Also there is no immunity until ten days or so after the injection. Once the puppy has fully recovered from the injection, i.e. after about ten days, you can start to lessen the number of meals per day.

First of all cut out the cereal at night, giving a little more supper and if possible an hour later. Then let the puppy sleep right through the night. After a week or so of this, cut out the midday meat and milk, but remember that, although the meals lessen in number, the food intake does not lessen, it grows. So add the food, some to the breakfast (i.e. the raw meat and milk) and some to the dinner in quantity. As the puppy grows, so the meals grow, although now only two in number, morning and evening. When the dog is six to eight months, it will get on to one big meal at night and will then remain on this one meal very strictly all its life.

There is one more thing you must do before the puppy is six months old, and that is to worm it again for roundworms (puppy worms). The breeder will have already done this once or twice before you took delivery. Your vet will give you a pill for this, or there are packets of pills you can get from any chemist if you ask for roundworm tablets. Tapeworms come when the dog is older and is running about on ground grazed by sheep or other animals, especially rabbits.

Keep a tin of flea or louse powder in the house, so that if the puppy rolls on a dead hedgehog, as dogs love to do, or carries a dead rabbit, or even sniffs down a rabbit hole, you can give it a good dusting to keep it free from any possible intruders, or mites picked up in the harvest field. You will need this powder

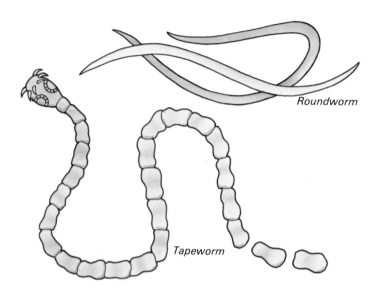

Roundworm

Tapeworm

Adult flea

Biting louse

Mite (microscopic)

Sucking louse

Engorged female tick

particularly if the dog is bedded on straw because straw harbours all sorts of tiny bugs and mites with which it can become infested. However, a good rubbing over with powder will keep it clean and this needs doing only occasionally.

To sum up, good food, plenty of water, rest, play and house training, its injections, its re-worming, and its powdering, and you are through the first vital six months.

Care of your Labrador from six months upwards

By the time your puppy is five months old, it will have been for some time on two meals a day, will have nearly finished teething, will have been re-wormed (or if not get that done now) and, most important, must have been inoculated against distemper and hardpad and probably, if you live in a dog-populated place such as a big village or suburb or even in a town where exercise takes place in a park, against the jaundice and liver diseases.

All that now remains is to keep the dog growing on well without becoming over-fat, to start giving it proper exercise and to get it properly trained. Having been inoculated, the dog can go about with you anywhere you wish. It still needs a small meal in the morning but will be having a big adult-type meal in the evening which, at about six months, will become its one and only meal of the day.

Basic training

The all-important thing now is to get the dog truly obedient, civilised and under your control at all times.

To start with you will need a safe place where you can shut the dog up if you want to go out without it, so I suggest you have a good, strong outside kennel with a run. Indeed, I like my dogs to sleep out of doors at night in such a kennel, even if they come into the house by day. In this way they soon get used to being in the kennel and will settle down with a big bone if you have to leave them. The big advantage of this is that there is no danger of their chewing up your cushions and curtains or your best eiderdown or duvet.

They are by nature terrible chewers, the 'mouthing' instinct being bred in them so that they feel they must employ their mouths. So when not actually retrieving or carrying something about in their mouths, they chew. I emphasise this, because you will need to recognise the fact. If your Labrador chews up something precious or some valuable document, it is your fault, not its fault. Its instinct is to do it and the way to avoid it happening is to remove chewable things when the dog is alone. So a good outdoor kennel is a very valuable thing in that the dog can be left alone in safety, with only its big marrow bone to chew.

I am very, very much against leaving Labradors to roam loose. Their working instincts are, as I say, destructive unless channelled into work itself, and their hunting instincts lead them into sheep and hen trouble unless watched and trained properly.

Like the mouthing and carrying instinct, this interest, indeed this obsession, with both livestock and birds is a necessity for the working side of the Labrador (and it is, and always must be, primarily a working dog), so you must direct this strong interest in 'fur and feather' into proper channels.

You must, in the maturing dog, teach it fully to understand and obey four important things:
1. To come right to you immediately you call it.
2. To walk to heel on a lead without pulling.
3. To walk to heel free without straying away.
4. To sit until told to move.

Unless you instil these into your puppy when it is only four or five months old, so that it *really* knows them and fully understands them, you are in for a lot of trouble, because a Labrador grows into a big, strong, boisterous and lively dog when still young, and only really settles down at about two years old. So get those lessons learned while the puppy is still small and weak enough for you to be on top, and it will then be a pleasant citizen, much easier to manage than it would have been if these lessons were left until later in life, when it might never learn them.

I teach my young puppies to come right up to me by sitting on my garden seat with a little hoard of 'goodies', pieces of cheese or cooked liver or small bits of biscuit. The puppy is allowed to play round me and at intervals I call it up and give it a little titbit and a good stroking and tickle under the tummy which dogs love. Then down it goes to play again, to be called up again and yet again for another snack. Cupboard love indeed, but they soon learn to come for the petting alone.

When, later, they go out in the fields for a walk off the lead, at intervals I give a whistle or call the name and *immediately* I turn and walk in another direction, changing the line of walk. The pup will soon realise that a whistle means, 'I'm changing direction, don't get left behind', and it will hurry after you. Again at intervals the puppy is called up for a pat and perhaps a little bit of biscuit or cheese, so it learns to come right up with alacrity.

One important point, *never, never* snub the puppy if it comes up to you. It may be bearing a nasty, stinking dead rabbit but it must *never* be slapped down on arrival. If you do this it may never come to you freely and with confidence again. Always greet your puppy with a pat and a kind word whenever and wherever it comes up to you to greet you.

Another thing you must never do is to take advantage of the puppy's confidence in you and, when it is doing something naughty, to call it up and then when it comes to you to catch it and smack or beat or shake it for its naughtiness. A puppy's logic is extremely primitive and simple. 'If I do wrong I am punished. I came right up to Master and was punished. Therefore I did wrong to come right up to him and got punished for doing it. I'll never be naughty and go up to him again.'

If a puppy leaves its naughtiness and comes up to you when you call, the right thing to do is to pat it and praise it for coming up and give it a titbit if you have one, as a reward. Then, without scolding, lead it to the scene of its crime and say 'No' to the actual wrong thing it was doing, making sure you completely divide into separate compartments in his mind the rightness of coming right up to you which gains a reward, and the wrongness of whatever he had been doing before.

Teach it each lesson quite separately. In this way your puppy will never be frightened of coming up to you, nor will it learn that maddening trick, that so many pet dogs have, of just keeping out of reach, so that you cannot catch it.

To teach the dog to walk to heel without pulling on the lead, put it on a tightish collar and lead. (Do not use a slip-lead or choke-chain which will tighten on its neck like a noose.) Then walk it along for a few steps. The dog will at first pull and struggle. It may go berserk with fright but try and jolly it along, loosening the pull whenever it gets too tight, rather like playing a salmon on rod and line. Pull and give, pull and give, and coax all the time trying to encourage it. The dog will usually walk quite well by the end of the first or perhaps the

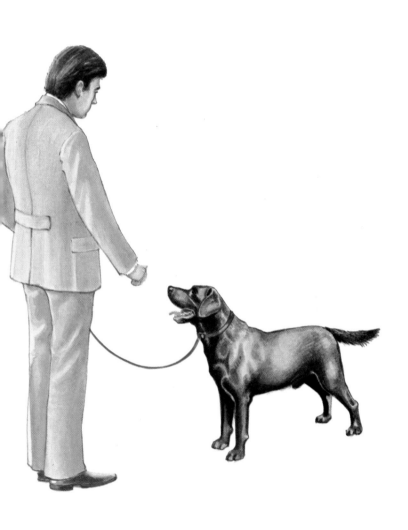

A chocolate Labrador in show stance

second time on the lead. Remember, any sort of choker is dangerous, as is a prolonged pull. So relax the pressure as soon as you can, at all times. Coax the dog to come with you.

Once the dog will walk on the lead, teach it not to pull. Take the dog to a path with a wall or hedge on your *left-hand* side. Walk it on the lead on your *left* against the wall. Whenever it tries to pass your knee to walk in front of you, give it a tap on the nose with a rolled newspaper or bushy, leafy twig. At the same time say with great emphasis, 'Heel'. The dog will get back behind your knee and, provided you then stop it from trying to cross behind you on to your right-hand side, it will soon learn to drop back to your left heel as soon as you say the word 'Heel'. It must also learn to keep there.

It is useful to walk it about between a row of chairs set on gravel or in your yard, or walk through obstacles like a gymkhana pony doing a bending-race. This makes the dog stick close to your heel and keep behind your left knee. When it has grasped this idea and is good at its figure of eight or bending-race round obstacles, then try it off the lead.

Another thing it can learn once it has learned to sit, is to walk forward at your heel, at first on its lead then later off the lead, and to sit while you walk away from it. Then suddenly call the dog up to heel but do not let it rush past you. It must 'heel up' properly. This is a very useful exercise, teaching the dog to listen, to concentrate, and to obey commands promptly.

Teaching a puppy to 'sit'

To teach it to sit, you can start while it is a very little puppy. As you say 'Sit' very firmly (but never shout at a Labrador, as they don't need or like it and it seems to depress them), press the puppy's behind down with one hand while raising its chin with the other. This forces it into the sit position. When it is sitting with your hand on its rump keeping it down, repeat the word 'sit' several times, raising your index finger at the dog. Then suddenly say, 'Come' or 'Here', whichever word you prefer, but choose one of these commands and always stick to it.

Let the dog jump up for a pat and a reward. Soon you will find that it starts to sink under your hand at the word 'sit', so that you will need only the pressure on its rump not the lift under the chin, and one day it will understand and will by itself sit on command. After this, prolong the time the dog sits before calling it up, and eventually you can walk a few steps away still using the raised finger and eventually raised hand command. In this way the dog will become obedient at the sit, so that you can drop it and leave it at the sit and walk away.

The dog will enjoy this exercise and will love the word 'here', rushing up to you to be congratulated on its cleverness. That is one great virtue of the Labrador. It loves learning a simple trick, and the agonising 'sit' gives way to the joyous rush of pleasure at being called up again and told how clever it has been. I am a great believer in praise for a dog. It loves it and it makes it feel very proud and 'wanted'.

I hate to see those (usually young) shooting men who are so self-conscious about their stiff upper lips and showing emotion. An older man will nearly always show a bit of pride in his dog, his self-consciousness having evaporated with maturity. These young men are so frightened of making fools of themselves that they will take a wonderfully and cleverly collected pheasant from their dog's mouth and, instead of congratulating it on its great cleverness and persistence and excellent retrieve and delivery to hand, will just turn on their heel without so much as a word of thanks to the poor Labrador which doesn't then know whether it did right or wrong. This I see often, both in young men and also in keepers when in front of other keepers, who they feel might 'rib' them for sentimentality.

I strongly believe that the dog should always know without any misunderstanding when it has done a good thing and

A home-made rope lead or check-cord can be used to teach a reluctant dog to 'come' and is a vital piece of equipment when teaching a dog to retrieve. If the dog either goes to retrieve before command or rushes past you on the retrieve, a foot can arrest the loose end of the lead.

when a bad. The only way is to praise when it does right and to scold when it does wrong. So, at the end of any exercise, give the dog its mead of praise and never, never snub or shake it if the most recent thing it has done is obeyed a command.

To sum up, between four and six months your puppy should have been inoculated, been re-wormed, got gradually on to two meals a day by six months and learned the basic lessons of 'sit', 'stay', 'come' (immediately when called), and to walk to heel both on the lead, and free, without pulling or going past your left knee. It is then well on the way to being a civilised dog.

Housing indoors and out

The question of housing, either indoors or out, or both at once, as many people with a pet Labrador do, is a difficult subject to write on, because every breeder will give you different advice according to their own circumstances, and you yourself will differ from the next owner in so far as your basic circumstances differ. So I can only give you the advice and help that is more or less general to all circumstances and must leave you yourself to sort it out according to your own financial position, the room available and whether you wish the dog to be indoors by day and outside at night, or indoors all the time, or a kennel dog. Few pet owners do this last thing, and indeed it is a difficult and rather hard method for the owners of a single house Labrador.

I can, however, lay down the chief principles which govern housing.

1. The kennel must be weatherproof if out of doors.
2. The accommodation whether inside or out must be as free as possible from draughts, as the slightest draught on a dog's back or stomach spells disaster either now or later in life.
3. The kennel must be cool in summer and warm and snug in winter.
4. There must be plenty of ventilation and any sleeping accommodation must not be near a coke boiler or any other form of fuel that can give off fumes. This means the garage for your car is completely unsuitable, as fumes even from a garaged car can kill.
5. The kennel must be light, and there must be no dark corners. Remember also that the dog wants to sleep, so it must not be too glaringly light or the dog will not settle. Use your common sense here.
6. The floor is important. It must be of a warm material such as wood, and must be easy to clean and keep dry. A sick dog must be in a place where it is possible to shut it to keep it completely quiet.
7. There must be a raised bed of proper size, draughtproof and snug. It must be made to keep bedding in, and to protect the dog's back, yet there must be easy access. On no account should the dog be allowed to sleep on the floor, even if it is wood, because draughts follow the floor-line.

These are the general principles to follow in all kennelling.

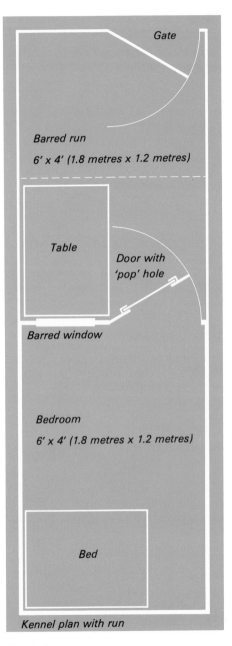

Gate

Barred run
6' x 4' (1.8 metres x 1.2 metres)

Roof to cover
half of run
for shelter

Table

Door with
'pop' hole

Barred window

Bedroom
6' x 4' (1.8 metres x 1.2 metres)

Bed

Kennel plan with run

38

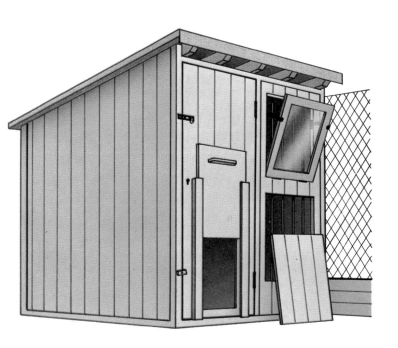

Kennel portion of accommodation, note the air space at the eaves

Also remember that if ill, the dog may cower right back into the farthest corner, so allow enough height for complete and easy access for yourself. Nothing is more irritating if you are anxious about a dog than for you and the vet continually to bump your head every time you stand up.

For indoor housing I suggest you decide in which room the dog is going to sleep, paying attention to the rule that the room must be only moderately warm, not icy cold and must be free from draughts and with a warm and cleanable floor. In this room I would put a good bed, preferably well raised from the floor and with a deep back and sides for protection from draughts. The front should be lower so as to allow easy access, but must also be high enough to keep the blanket in.

The blanket should be folded and if possible tucked in for the dog to lie on, and a couple of folded newspapers placed underneath it to act as underblankets. Put this bed in the most draughtproof and cosy place in the room, although I do *not* advise any artificial heat, partly because of a Labrador's very thick coat and also because of the danger from fumes. If your dog's bed is in the kitchen where there is a solid fuel stove, then again beware of fumes. As coke and anthracite fumes lie a few inches deep at floor level, raise the bed 5-6in. (13-15cm.) and stuff something underneath it. In this way, your puppy will be able to get up into the bed and will be prevented from crawling underneath. If there is no danger of fumes in the room, the bed needs to be raised only about 2in. (5cm).

You can, from the very first day, make your puppy sleep in this one room, removing all carpets of course at first, and also curtains and cushions, a puppy's favourite playthings. Keep the bed in the same place and let the puppy rest there after its meals and exercise.

As well as this bed in one room, which may be a kitchen, a downstairs cloakroom or a small spare room or office, it is advisable to have a folding dog bed in the sitting room or a blanket on an armchair that the dog is allowed to use during the day when you are there with it. Also have a blanket or bench in the room where you eat. These temporary beds are for when the dog is with you in the daytime.

If the dog's actual 'bedroom' is too cold in winter, you can substitute a covered box for its open bed, but if you do this, you *must* put it in the same place and see that the dog has taken to it. They hate a new bed at first and some Labradors will never sleep in a covered bed. But if your dog will take to it, then a big crate on its side makes a good bed, and if necessary you can, on bitter nights, nail a sack over the opening so that the dog can push it to and fro to enter. But remember it will not understand this at first and therefore must be taught how to use the opening by pushing the sack aside. A night-bed, a day-bed, and perhaps a blanket or two are all the housing needed indoors.

For a dog that lives outside or is outside at night, I would suggest you need only the day-bed and the couple of blankets in the house, but for outside a proper warm kennel with a good chain link or railed run must be provided. I will describe this kennel in full. I like it 6ft. (1.8m.) high at the *front* of the wooden kennel (or if you have a stone potting shed, that is very handy). The inside of the kennel must be at least 4ft. by 6ft. (1.2m. by 1.8m.) giving a single dog 24sq.ft. (2.24 sq.m.) of floor space. This is the minimum size laid down per single dog in the Dog Breeders Act.

A bed for use inside outdoor accommodation

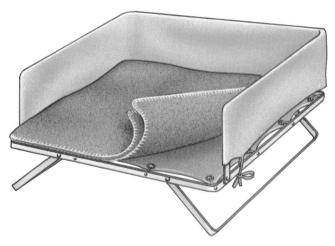

A canvas folding bed for home use

41

I do *not* like a cement or stone floor for the sleeping compartment as cold strikes up from the floor through the first 2ft. (61cm.) of air, so that the chill reaches the dog even in a raised bed. I therefore like a wood floor or tight-packed earth or sand. The kennel must be waterproof and draughtproof. There must be a window that can be opened and I always have a barred grid over it, so that I can leave it wide open on hot, stuffy nights and know that the dog will not be able to jump out. Glass by itself is not safe. I've known a Labrador or two jump right through glass with disastrous results.

There should be only *one* door in the kennel because of draughts. This door must be able to be opened from the inside in case the dog knocks the door shut and you get trapped, but the catch must be high enough for the dog not to be able to knock it open from the inside by jumping up. A bolt on the outside is handy because then the dog cannot slam the door and fasten it with you inside.

Again, I like a strong bolt on the outside of the door, so that the dog cannot work it loose. Also remember to turn the bolt down into one of the slots for the purpose, so that the dog cannot work it loose by shaking the door.

Attached to the kennel there should be a run made of chain link or weldmesh. I prefer the latter because, if of fairly heavy gauge, the dog cannot chew through it or pull it loose or make it sag by jumping at it.

This run should be 6ft. (1.8m.) high, 4ft. (1.2m.) wide to match the measurement of the wooden kennel given above, and at least 6ft. (1.8m.) long or preferably 8ft. (2.4m.), giving the dog a run of either 24 or 32sq.ft. (2.24 or 3sq.m.). This outside run should be of concrete. I also roof-over half the length of this run and put a small bench under the half-roofing so that the dog can sit outside in its run under shelter on a wettish day. It must have access at all times to its sleeping compartment which contains its bed. The bed should be large enough for the dog to stretch right out on it, and if out of doors, must be made of a material that the dog cannot tear to bits, i.e. wood. This is because a dog sleeping outside is much more likely to chew than an indoor family dog, simply through loneliness and often boredom.

There must be a good door on the outside run, with a strong fastener, and again remember to see that you can open it from the inside. I wonder how many times I've let people out of their

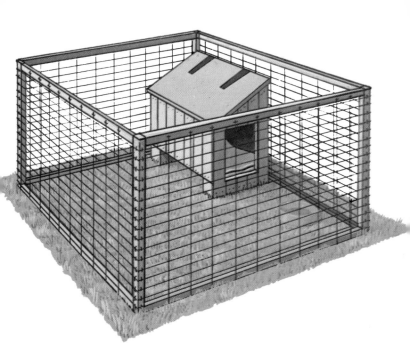

A puppy pen should have an area of shade, accommodation off the ground and water always available

own dog runs, and I myself have twice been caught, so learned the lesson the hard way.

Usually the run door opens inwards so that a dog cannot rush you and knock it open and you down as you open it. But this is a disadvantage if you live in a very snowy district. After a heavy fall of snow you may find you are unable to open the run door, and as the run is 6ft. (1.8m.) high, you will certainly not be able to clamber over to dig the snow away. For this reason I have any door or gate that I can't reach over made to open outwards (the wrong way) just for snow. Of course the kennel door need not open outwards because it presumably will not snow inside the actual kennel. But just think of this point when you erect a kennel-run and decide for yourself, according to whether you are much troubled by heavy snow.

If you follow this advice and have a sound kennel supplied with a good bed and floor, leading to an outside day-run, then you will not only have somewhere where the dog can sleep at night if you so choose, but you will also have somewhere safe for it to be if you have to go out and leave it for an hour or two at home by itself. In that case see that it has a good marrow bone to chew while shut up, so that it is not tempted to chew its bed or the kennel. The dog may still do this because the instinct to use its mouth is so strong, but at least it will be chewing mendable wood and not your best drawing room carpet.

My ideal outside kennel (unless it is one of those useful potting shed buildings I have already mentioned) is a wooden kennel built by one of the many experienced kennel-builders whose names can be obtained from the dog papers. This will be purpose built and will have a big door for your use and a small pop-hole for the dog's use, both of which can be either shut or fastened open. There will be an openable window and I also like a removable shutter with a barred aperture so that the dog can be left in the kennel if it is ill or if the weather is really desperate such as deep snow or thunder storms, and still see out and get all the air it needs. There is nothing so boring for a dog as to be shut for hours behind closed doors with no outlook. This leads to all sorts of vices such as constant barking and tearing everything up in its desperation.

A dog loves to see what is going on. Let the dog enjoy itself as much as it can, even if it has sometimes to be shut up completely. Let the dog have light, air, a nice run, a warm bed, a good view of life outside, and a big marrow bone to take the

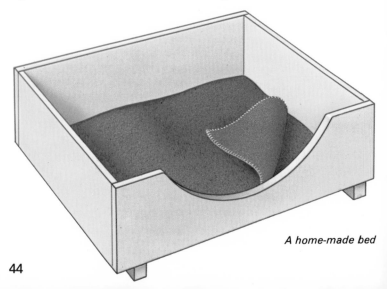

A home-made bed

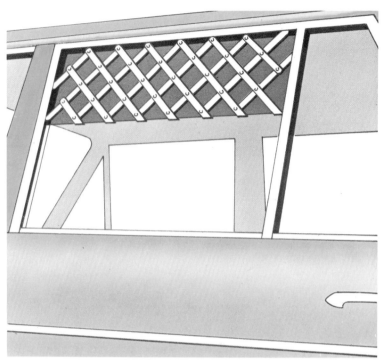

Even when using a trellis frame window vent, do not park your car in direct sunlight.

mischief out of its idle teeth, and you are more likely to have a good dog than if it is in a darkened, viewless, 'nothing-to-do' prison.

Do not kennel your dog in the car or estate car. Here lies an unexpected danger. A standing car, even with the engine turned off, may still seep exhaust fumes during the night. These have collected in such places as the boot and other cavities and as the car gets warm with the heat of the dog asleep, these fumes are released and spread up into the body of the car. Get a proper kennel and run, and let the dog think of it as its other home and it will then be content if you have to leave it for an hour or two. Your mind will be at rest and at least it will not be your Labrador who killed all those hens while you were at the dentist. You will know that the dog is safe and it will be resting, because active Labradors need more sleep than many people realise, especially as puppies.

Grooming

Grooming divides into two sections, home grooming and grooming for shows, the second depending on the first and both depending largely on how correctly and well the dog is fed.

Home grooming

Every dog that lives in the house as a family pet should have its everyday attention and brushing, not only for its own comfort but also for the safety, comfort and hygiene of the family. Dogs that are about to be shown need just that little bit extra as the great day approaches. But if the diet is correct and the dog has occasionally had the necessary regular dusting against possible fleas or other parasites that it may pick up in its daily rounds, then little more than a brush and comb-through is needed, even for the show ring.

First let us take the ordinary house pet, which needs watching carefully for signs of scratching and unease. The tools for the job are a soft brush, a hard brush, a comb, preferably metal with large teeth at one end and small at the other (this can be bought at any pet shop and should be strong for a Labrador), and a clean duster. In addition, but not strictly necessary, I like a chamois leather, such as is used for washing cars and windows, and I always keep handy a blunt-ended pair of surgical scissors.

If the dog is dry and clean, all that is needed daily is a brushing all over with the soft brush followed by a polish with the duster. No other tool is necessary for this ordinary routine grooming, which makes the dog feel comfortable and trim and gives it a nice polish. When the dog comes in wet and muddy from a walk, dip the chamois leather in clean water, and wring it as dry as you can. Then use this to dry the dog all over, squeezing the leather out at intervals (and you will be astonished at how much you can squeeze out). You will find that the chamois leather, which has much the same effect as the dog's own tongue, will absorb all the water and the dog will become quite dry after a good rub over.

Give the dog time to dry off completely, then immediately wipe off any remaining dry mud with the hard brush, otherwise it may clog the coat and be difficult to remove. This is the usual purpose of the hard brush. The other use of the hard brush with the comb is when the dog starts to shed its coat, when a good combing, using both the large and small teeth, followed by a good brushing with the hard brush, helps to remove those terrible hairs into the dustbin and not on to the carpet and chair covers. A tremendous lot of coat comes off at these times, taking days and days to come out, but you can speed up the process by this vigorous use of the comb and hard brush, if possible twice a day while the coat-cast is on.

Once the coat is out and the new coat showing through, you can go back to the daily soft brushing without the comb, polishing with the duster and using the hard brush and chamois leather only when the coat is wet or muddy. In this way your dog's coat will stay clean, polished and healthy, indeed fit for humans to touch.

I do advise you, though this is not strictly speaking grooming, to watch how you touch other dogs. Do not pat any dog that comes up to you, because skin disease in many cases is very catching and can be transferred to your dog on your hand. Other dogs may not be as clean and hygienic as your own, and under no circumstances touch a dog with bare patches, wrinkled skin or spots.

The daily routine of brushing and polishing gives you a chance to look at ears, eyes and toenails, and to watch for cuts, thorns or cracked pads and to deal with them accordingly. Remember that even the cleanest of dogs may at any time pick up skin parasites, even from a perfectly clean and healthy harvest field. The dog can get cat-fleas, rabbit-fleas, harvest mites, cattle lice and there is no shame in it. It's just a dog's life and, as someone once said, gives it (and you) something to think about.

One elderly, very house-proud Labrador owner told me that she fainted clean out at the vet's surgery when he told her that all that was wrong with her dog was that it had caught a flea.

Keep a tin of a good dog's insecticide and use it. Once again your friendly pet shop will tell you what is good and safe. Then just occasionally, say once a month, or immediately if your dog starts to scratch with its teeth at its paws or flanks, dust it over, rubbing the powder well into the coat. If that does not stop the itching, tell your vet. It is not likely to be anything more than a chance 'visitor' probably picked up in straw, but if in doubt then ask your vet, but don't faint away when he tells you, 'It's only a flea'.

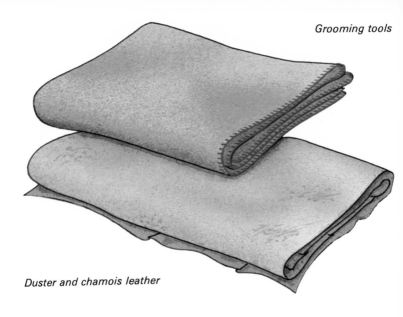

Grooming tools

Duster and chamois leather

Soft brush

Hard bristle brush

Steel comb

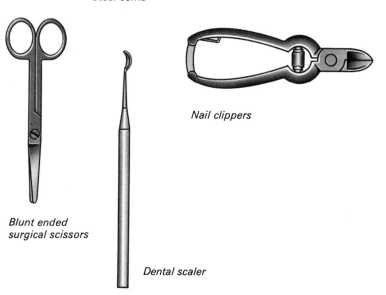

Nail clippers

*Blunt ended
surgical scissors*

Dental scaler

Although not strictly speaking actual grooming, I keep an eye on the whole dog at the same time. I look at the toenails to see that they are in trim, particularly the dew claws, those little toes half way up the lower front leg. These claws are often left on in Labradors to help their work over walls and up and down slopes. Some dogs use them in hilly country and keep them worn short, but in most dogs they are rudimentary and completely unused, so possibly they may grow round into the dog's leg or break off most painfully.

Be prepared to clip the toenails yourself with a strong pair of clippers, which some people hate doing, or take the dog to the vet to be done, although the dog seems to hate this even more than you do cutting them yourself. They have to be done, if they are growing too long, so make your decision. Do not put it off or you may cause the dog great pain if they grow too long. I

Clipping a puppy's nails

do them myself and my dogs don't seem to mind, because I've done it since puppyhood and never hurt them, so they do not fear it and find nothing strange about it.

The ears also need watching to see if they are getting a dirty, rusty discharge inside, or if they smell. I keep a regular canker powder at hand and will deal with the treatment of the ear and give the recipe for canker powder in the chapter on Health.

A point that is often forgotten or not known is that the dog has two anal glands (scent-glands), under the tail. In some dogs these need squeezing out at intervals. If the dog toboggans on the ground or bites at its tail-root, tries to reach its tail, chases it or gets a patchy coat over the hind regions, it may be one of two things, worms or anal glands. I have learned to squeeze my own dogs' glands, having been shown how to do it by my vet, and so can you. But if you don't fancy this rather messy, smelly job, then ask your vet about it, if you suspect it needs doing.

The other thing I watch at all times is eye-cleanness. But as this is a subject on its own, I will deal with it in the chapter on Health.

Grooming for show
If the diet is correct and the coat kept in good condition by daily care and attention as I have already described, then little more

needs to be done to get the dog in show coat, provided, of course, that it is not shedding its coat, in which case it is little use showing the animal till the new coat is in.

The day before the show give a real good brush with the soft brush and then polish extra hard with the duster. Myself, I do not like to use the comb before showing because I am a great believer that a true Labrador has a built-in undercoat and that, even in a hot climate, this undercoat is and should be present. So do not comb till it is all out, and above all, unless you are forced to do so with a yellow or cream-coloured dog, do not bath the dog the day before the show. This may be necessary several days before if the dog is really town-stained and grubby, but it should not be necessary at all. While you are doing your soft brushing and polishing, look to see if the tail needs trimming at the very tip. Usually a Labrador needs no trimming at all, but the tail naturally has about 1-1½in. (2.5-3.8cm.) of hair on the extreme tip.

It is usual, provided the dog has a nice normal length of true Labrador's tail, to trim off this extra length of hair so that the tail looks short. But do this so that the point still looks as natural as possible, i.e. taper it off with your blunt surgical scissors. I often carry a curved pair in my show bag just for the purpose of shaping the tip to a nice point, having made the tail a good 1in. (2.5cm.) shorter than with the hair left on. I must make it plain that it is only the hair that is shortened. Great care must be taken not to damage the tip of the tail itself even if only very slightly, because a tail is a delicate thing carrying an artery, and a cut tip can cause really excessive and frightening bleeding. So always use surgical scissors with the blunt tips so that you make no mistake.

The above instructions cover all the pre-show grooming or trimming required by a Labrador, one of the easiest dogs to prepare for show, provided it is fit and well.

When you arrive at the show give your dog a good grooming with the soft brush and the duster. Let the dog rest till just before it is due in the ring, when you give it a really good and thorough going over again with the soft brush and duster. For the show itself slip on a thin light lead (made specially for the purpose), and the dog is ready, although I always take my brush and duster to the ringside, in case I feel I need it.

One word of warning. What I have described above is all that is necessary. Do not, *please*, get into the habit of brushing,

brushing and better brushing. You will see owners of other breeds, notably Afghans and Pekes, doing this perfectly unnecessarily, even while in the ring. It is really more a nervous habit than anything. They see others doing it and they copy it. I feel sorry for these poor dogs. Labradors do not need this and one good brushing and polishing just before entry into the ring is sufficient.

Exhibiting and show training

Before you start to show I advise you to find out from your pet shop the name and address of your local or nearest canine society and to contact the secretary. He or she will tell you whether the club is holding any ring training classes or any match meetings, as small social evenings are called, where you can take your dog into the ring to get it used to the atmosphere and the idea of being looked at and handled all over by a stranger, and walked up and down the ring.

Showing is an art that needs to be learned, although it is not difficult to master. But for the dog, which must be six months old before it can enter a real show, it is a great ordeal at first. The crowded room, the masses of other puppies, some bold, some scared, the attention it gets from friendly people and the fact of a total stranger looking at its teeth and its testicles is very strange. The dog soon gets to know the job as well as you do, but I like a small happy affair to start it off and not a real show.

If you can find one, take the dog to a ringcraft class or two first, and if possible to a match meeting. Otherwise, ask where there are any small local shows, without too high an entry fee, so that the dog does not throw away too much money the first few times if it cowers from the judge, or refuses to trot up and down the ring, as it may very well do.

Your pet shop will have supplies of schedules of your local shows, or you can get one from the secretary of the show. Read the schedule most carefully from cover to cover, and I mean literally every word the first few times, until you know the rules by heart and what to look for. It gives, most important, the date, place and time of the show and also very important, the last date for sending entries. Secretaries are very strict. By Kennel Club ruling, they must not take late entries, so find out those two dates and send your entries in good time.

At first, until you and the dog both have the hang of showing, enter only a very few classes, sticking to the puppy classes, the 'Maiden' and the 'Novice'. Your schedule will tell you clearly the meanings of these classes.

Puppy and Junior classes depend on age, but remember the dog must be six months old to enter at all. 'Maiden' and 'Novice' depend on whether the dog has ever won a first prize, or how many firsts it has already won.

There is one misleading definition which reads 'Open, for all dogs'. This does not mean that you have to enter all dogs at the show in this class. It means that any dog can enter whatever its age or wins, so all the top dogs and famous ones will be in it. Do not bother to enter this class until you know your dog is a good specimen and of top class from the show point of view.

I must also remind you that you are showing the *dog* and not its pedigree, however good the pedigree is. I say this because so many newcomers to showing think that, because their pet has a long pedigree well spotted with champions, this alone makes it a show dog. This unfortunately is not so. It is the dog itself that counts and how it is constructed.

A show dog has to have certain points and requirements and the best bred dog may be lacking in some of these. Judges and breeders can recognize these points instantly, but as yet it is difficult for you to do so and will be probably for several years. You do not either learn or win prizes by staying at home, so, if you think your dog a better than usual Labrador, try it out a couple of times and see if the judges think so too.

Do not lash out too much entry money at first until you get to know the dog's form. Try one or two different judges and if the dog fails to win, ask a good breeder about it.

On the other hand, if it is pulled out even for a Very Highly Commended, then give the dog some more chances to see if it really is a show specimen. If it is, you will have fun, good days, bad days, heartache and jubilation. No one can say the show ring is a dull place with its ups and down, triumphs and disappointments. If after persistent trying a breeder advises you that the dog really is not a show specimen, then remember that it is still a lovely dog, exactly the same dog you took to the show in the morning. Your pet has not deteriorated during the day just because the judge does not think it a show specimen. It still has all the good points of sweet nature, affection for you and everything else that it started the day with, and you can still be just as proud and fond of the dog as before.

If you do decide to go on showing, you will need a few extra pieces of equipment. The dog's usual collar and lead will take it to the show, but a nice, light show-slip, which is a decorative lead with a noose of some sort instead of a collar, is needed for showing. These show-slips vary in heaviness, colour, texture and actual design, but your pet shop will help you with this,

A yellow Labrador

and you can always ask the breeder of your pup or a friend used to showing Labradors. Remember that what is right for a Pug, Peke or Great Dane is not right for a Labrador. They have their own weight and thickness of show-slip, so choose this type with someone else's help.

If you are going to a bigger show where the dogs are to be benched (your schedule will carry the words 'benched' or 'unbenched' unless it is a Championship Show, for these shows are always benched for Labradors), you will need a collar and chain. The collar must be stout, strong and fit fairly tightly. You *must* ask advice about the chain, if you do not know the type required, because this is a special benching chain with a clip at each end, two swivels and several rings inserted up and down the full length, so an ordinary chain will not do. You must buy the correct sort which is laid down in Kennel Club rules.

Once you really start showing, you should fit up a bag with a zip fastener with all these essentials: show-slips, bench-chains, stout collar, a water dish, deep and light, and your soft brush, your hard brush, in case the dog gets muddy by any chance, your duster and your blunt scissors. A couple of big safety pins will be needed, one for your ring number and one as a spare. Having duly sent in your entries before the closing date, off you go to the show whether or not you have received any tickets or further notification whatsoever.

Benching chain

Your ring training class will have taught your dog three basic things:
1. To stand up on the lead and look up at a titbit (usually cooked liver that you have prepared the day before, cut small and carried in a small greaseproof bag in your pocket). The dog will look intelligent if properly trained for show and will wag its tail. A dog is always examined by the judge standing up, so do

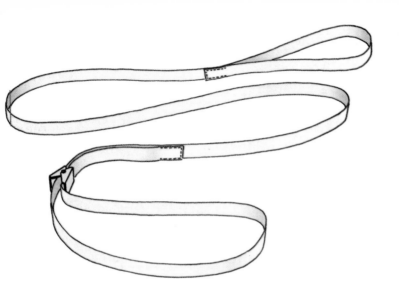

A slip lead

An alternative show lead

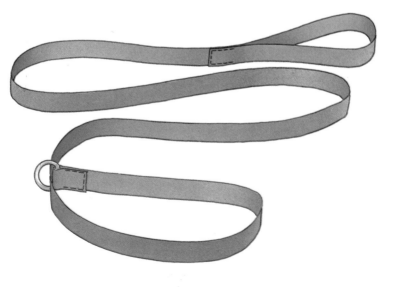

57

A section of show benching

not say 'Sit' as soon as you reach the judge. Keep the dog standing.

2. The dog will have learned to have its teeth looked at with its mouth tightly closed, so that the judge can see he has a proper scissor-bite. Also, if a dog, it will have got used to having its testicles handled by the judge, a necessary thing in the English show ring, because the dog must have two fully descended testicles.

3. The dog will have learned to trot up and down the ring at a smooth pace by your side, going straight and not pulling on the lead to the side.

That is all the basic training it needs for the show ring. If you have any doubt as to whether the dog will do these things correctly, get your friends to handle it all over and look at its teeth by just turning the lips back, and yourself trot the dog up and down a few paces until it gets practised at this easy exercise.

Having given the dog its last brush and polish, enter the ring when your first class is called. Keep your ears open for this because it is your responsibility to be in the ring at the right moment, not anyone else's. At one time the steward was responsible for collecting the class together, but now the onus of getting into the ring is entirely on you.

As a Novice you should always stand in the middle of the line until you get into the swing of showing, so that, whichever end the judge starts with, you will be able to watch the routine and follow it exactly. In your turn, the judge will call you up to him, will handle your dog from tip to toes, including its teeth, etc., as you have already practised. He will then ask you to move the dog, which means trotting it up and down at a smart pace, either straight to the judge or in a triangle, whichever he asks you to do. The show ring diagrams illustrate these two movements. Then you go back to your place and wait until he calls you again, if he wants to see you further. That is all that is required in the ring, but, as I say, watch the others so as to get the idea, thus saving time for the judge. Keep cool and remember that you need not have stage fright. No one is looking at you, only at your dog and it does not mind. If you are entered in more than one class, again keep your ears and eyes open because if you happen to miss a class you may have all your prizes taken away.

You will find that, although the other exhibitors are very busy with their own dogs, they will be glad to help you if you do not understand something or are lost in any way. You may feel a bit strange at first, but within a few weeks there will be someone coming into the ring for the first time and you yourself will be telling them what to do and helping them like an old hand.

"New" dogs (unseen by Judge)

Handler
Dog being examined by Judge
Judge

"Old" dogs (already seen by Judge in a previous class)

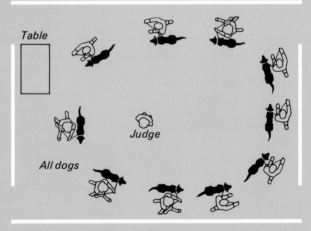

Table

Judge

All dogs

"Once round, please"

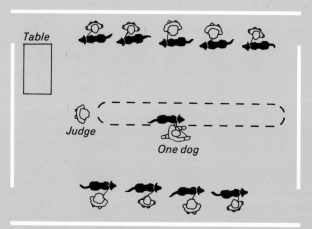

"Once up and down, please"

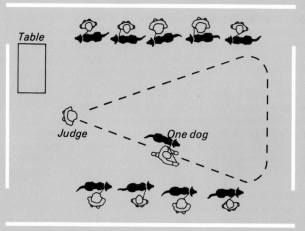

"Triangle, please"

61

Colour in the Labrador

The British Breed Standard describes the colour of the Labrador as 'Generally black or yellow, but other whole colours are permitted'. Note that they do not call the yellow Labrador 'golden'. This is because of an edict made by the Kennel Club many years ago when the Golden Retriever (a totally different breed from a different hemisphere, originating in Middle Europe, while the Labrador came from Canada) became popular. Confusion arose between the Golden Labrador and the Golden Retriever, so the Kennel Club wisely allotted the word 'yellow' to the Labrador breed and 'golden' to the Golden Retriever exclusively. This is correct usage, and if you see an advertisement for 'Golden' Labradors for sale you may be sure that the seller does not know the first thing about the breed and therefore is not really safe to buy from. If he is as ignorant as this about the actual name of the breed, he is likely to be even more ignorant about rearing puppies, not knowing whether they are good or bad ones, and unable to recognise other more difficult but necessary attributes of the breed.

Yellow covers all shades of biscuit, cream, mustard or red and all these colours are allowed and come under the heading 'yellow'. Blacks explain themselves, and the only other colour at the present moment in the Labrador is chocolate, also called liver. It was found by the breeders of this colour that liver was not an acceptable word to the pet buyer, but that chocolate was a much more attractive term. Chocolates are a true chocolate brown and once seen cannot be confused with the deepest yellow, even in the nest. The terms liver and chocolate are the same and interchangeable.

Colour inheritance between black and yellow is very easily explained. I am not here going into difficult technical terms, but will state the simple Mendelian principle of Dominant (black) and Recessive (yellow). This is exactly the same as in the old limerick when, marrying black to white, 'The result of their sins was quadruplets not twins, one black, one white and two khaki'. Except that in Labradors, the result of mating a black to a cream (or any shade of yellow) is two blacks and two yellows and four, which, instead of being khaki, are black in colour but bear a hidden yellow gene in their inheritance.

Blacks bearing the yellow genes of inheritance will always appear exactly the same black as the 'pure' blacks and can be

A black Labrador

discovered only by what they throw when mated to a selection of bitches, including a good few yellows. An expert can also deduce their inheritance from their pedigree, in many cases.

The 'pure' black can only produce blacks to any yellow, whether cream or darker yellow; the blacks carrying the yellow gene sire a few yellows in every litter unless mated to a 'pure' black.

The simple chart overleaf explains this expectancy.

Chocolate is a more difficult colour to breed with any certainty. There are various types of brown colouring which is what causes the difficulty. For example, a chocolate with yellow eyes and pink eyelids and nose is a different genetic colouring from a dark deep brown with dark amber eyes, and deep brown nose and eye rims. Another difficulty is that chocolate is a 'dilute' colour acting as an alternative dominant to black over yellow but as a recessive to black and a dominant to yellow, this being a triple complication. So chocolate mated to chocolate produces a different coloured chocolate from those produced by mating a chocolate to a black carrying a chocolate gene, and again to a chocolate-yellow mating, all these producing different ratios of puppies of differing hereditary pattern from the others.

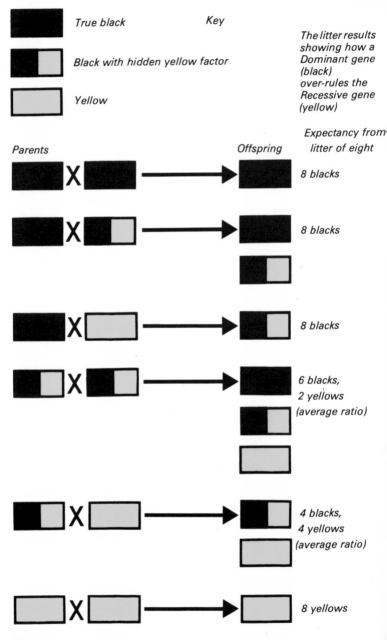

Key

True black

Black with hidden yellow factor

Yellow

The litter results showing how a Dominant gene (black) over-rules the Recessive gene (yellow)

Parents

Offspring

Expectancy from litter of eight

X → 8 blacks

X → 8 blacks

X → 8 blacks

X → 6 blacks, 2 yellows (average ratio)

X → 4 blacks, 4 yellows (average ratio)

X → 8 yellows

So the lot of the chocolate breeder is very hard compared to those interested in blacks and yellows, where you can breed just about what you like.

Unfortunately, most combinations of chocolate and the other two colours produce more bad coloured chocolates with light eyes than correct ones, and I have yet to meet a breeder who could say what they were going to produce in any unborn litter. They just keep their fingers crossed that they may produce one, if only one, good coloured, correctly pigmented chocolate with good coloured eyes.

Because of these difficulties, good chocolates are few and far between, as are good breeders of this strange colour. The best advice I can give you if you want to breed chocolates is to learn slightly more about colour-inheritance than you need for the other two easier colours. Pick the brains of a good chocolate breeder before you start on any mating to produce the colour, and keep introducing blacks carrying the chocolate genes so as to try and darken your colour to dark chocolate, avoiding 'Milk Chocolate' or 'Chocolate Crisps' as the light, ginger-brown, gooseberry-eyed, pink-pigmented Labradors are known in some overseas countries. To be a good chocolate Labrador it *must* have the deep colour, the attractive eye and the correct pigmentation, as well as all the usual good points of a show Labrador.

The reason that there have been only two chocolate champions in Britain is because of the above difficulties of eye colour and pigmentation, although the chocolate illustrated on page 16 is well on the way to becoming the third champion.

Breeding

I am going to surprise you in this chapter by starting with the words 'do not' though I had better add 'That is unless you have some very good reason to do so'. From long and bitter experience I am strongly of the opinion that breeding Labradors should be left to the breeders. But if you wish to join their ranks properly with the idea of carrying on a breeding and showing (or working) kennels, doing it correctly from the word go, when you should read a more advanced book than this (see the Reading List at the end of the book), then I will help you all I can with your venture.

Some reasons why you might feel you want to breed a litter are:

Perhaps as a replacement of some dear old soul whose excellent character you want to carry on into another generation.

You may feel your bitch is too slim in body and if you wish to show her next year, you think a litter might mature her.

You may have heard that it 'steadies her up' and makes her less snappy, disobedient or wild. (That is a *bad* reason. Never set out to perpetuate these faults which may easily be inherited.)

If you are told she *must* be bred from sometime during her life, then that too is no longer necessary.

It certainly was true when I was first breeding Labradors and then we were apt to lose them from womb trouble unless we did. But your vet with his magic antibiotics can take care of this nowadays, so do not breed a litter just for this reason.

You may breed a litter by mistake. Many pets get 'caught' and if the 'lover' was a Labrador then you may feel inclined to go on with it. If the dog was *not* a Labrador, then I advise you to get the vet to inject your bitch just as soon as you possibly can, to prevent the unwanted litter. I believe this has to be done at once, or not more than a day after the mating.

The last reason is to make money, and this is the worst reason of all because you may actually lose a lot of money instead. Breeding a litter of pups is a *very* costly business both in money and time and usually the pet 'breeder' sighs with relief as some professional breeder feels sorry for her and takes the last puppies away.

So think, think, and think again, and if you have now decided

Yellow puppies with their mother. Yellow covers all shades of biscuit, cream, mustard or red

to go ahead, I will not attempt to dissuade you further but will try to help you in your trouble, sorrow, sickness (the puppies, not you) and lots and lots of other adversities, so that perhaps you will not encounter quite so many of the possible snags.

First of all you must wait until the bitch is old enough. I suggest that you breed from her any time between seventeen months and three and a half years. That is indeed perhaps rather late in her life and I would advise sooner, not later. She should not be started as a mother after three and a half years or you may run into trouble, and again not sooner than her second season at least. So if she is over her first season and is about sixteen or seventeen months at her second 'heat', that is the time to start her. Of course, if she has previously bred a litter, she can go on doing so until about seven years old, but it is important that she is not bred from twice in a year. Miss a season every time if you possibly can.

Having decided this, the next thing is to choose a stud dog. Do *not* choose the dog next door, I beg you, unless he is something super himself. If you want to get the puppies to pay

The genital organs

Dog

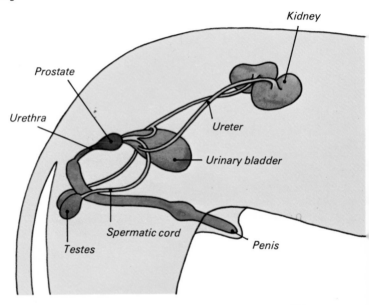

Kidney

Prostate

Urethra

Ureter

Urinary bladder

Spermatic cord

Testes

Penis

Bitch

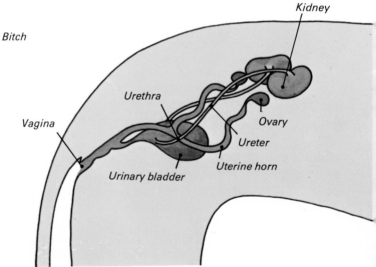

Kidney

Urethra

Vagina

Ovary

Ureter

Uterine horn

Urinary bladder

for themselves or perhaps even make a small profit, then you *must* use a known stud dog with a famous reputation. Get the names and all details of some of the famous dogs, or better still ask the breeder of your puppy to advise on a suitable dog. Then write or ring the dog owner and ask whether he or she will accept your bitch to their dog (you have no right to demand to use a dog even if advertised at stud). Tell the owner when the bitch is due in season, usually about six and a half months after she was in before, and do not forget to tell the stud dog owner her pedigree to make sure that the dog is not too close-bred to your bitch's bloodlines. Also ask the fee, because this varies and you must be able to pay the full amount due *at the time the mating takes place.*

As the time draws near, watch your bitch very carefully for signs of the season starting, i.e. the bitch licking herself a lot, spots of blood on her bedding and the floor, a lot of penny-spending of tiny amounts of urine and a gradual swelling of the vulva. As soon as you see the signs of blood-spotting, tell the dog owner who will tell you when to come, usually about the twelfth to fourteenth day. You will take the bitch to the dog, unless another arrangement is made, but dog owners usually prefer their studs to work on their own ground. This is because the dog must have full confidence in his surroundings; so be prepared to travel with your bitch.

Even before the bitch is in season, indeed as soon as you know you are going ahead with a litter, write to the Kennel Club (the address is given at the end of the book), and ask for an application form for registering a litter. This is a green form, Kennel Club Form No. 1. When you go to the stud dog take this form with you and see that the owner of the dog signs it as soon as the mating is over and when you are paying your fee.

You will have been watching your bitch carefully ever since she started to 'stain', as we call the blood-spots. Towards the tenth or eleventh day this discharge should turn thick, and then start to dry up and the bitch should switch her tail to one side if you tickle her back at the root of the tail. When she turns her tail up and to one side she is ready for mating.

It is essential you should understand the mating of dogs. After the dog has mounted the bitch successfully, a 'tie' will take place. The dog owner will turn the dog so that he and the bitch stand firmly fixed, back to back. You will hold her head and the dog owner will see to the dog. This 'tie' lasts from as little as a minute up to twenty minutes or half an hour. So when you take the bitch give yourself several hours for the whole performance and *do not bring the children* because you will be thoroughly busy and will be quite unable to keep an eye on bored children who may get up to mischief. I speak from experience here.

When eventually the 'tie' comes loose, take the bitch back to the car in which you brought her and then pay your fee to the owner. You will collect the dog's pedigree, his K.C. numbers, and will get your K.C. form signed and filled in with the dog's name and number.

Take your bitch home and watch her as carefully as you did before, for another week or ten days at least. She is still vulnerable to other dogs, and you can only register her litter as by your chosen dog if no other dog has got at her either before or after mating. Do not try and cheat in any way over this, because if you used the stud dog *after* another dog had already got at her, when the pups came you would be liable to be prosecuted under the Trades Description Act if you tried to sell them with the 'good' dog's pedigree. Remember that the stud dog owner can tell if the puppies are by his dog or if another had already mated the bitch.

Keep the bitch quiet for the rest of the day, and before you leave the breeder's kennels, ask the owner of the stud dog whether she needs a second mating by the dog a couple of days later. This is not usually necessary. The next day, the bitch goes back to her normal 'in season' routine for the next week or more until she is completely 'off season'. Then she goes on as before, but as she gets heavy take her off strenuous work and do not allow jumping or swimming. But she must have some exercise to keep her muscles right for whelping, so see she gets regular suitable exercise for a 'mum-to-be'.

Do not alter her food directly after she is mated, but see later on that she gets very good food and plenty of it. If she gets too heavy you could divide her one meal into two, so that she eats night and morning instead of just at night. This may help her bear her burden more easily.

Ten days before whelping, get her box and 'place' ready. I illustrate an open whelping box for an indoor whelping, and one for an outdoor kennel, if the weather is very cold, with a sack over the entrance.

Give her plenty of newspapers to whelp on, before she starts

Whelping box

to whelp, which will be sixty to sixty-three days after the mating (the normal time being exactly nine weeks, but bitches can whelp up to five days early or two or three days late). She will start fussing, panting, looking wild and generally creating a fuss and bother of moving boxes, chewing wood, etc. This means she is starting, and she will refuse her food and drink while this performance is on.

She will get more and more restive, and I like to watch her closely as time goes on. Eventually, she will lie down and start to strain. After some time she will make a super effort and out should slide the first puppy. She will probably turn on it very quickly and start to open the bag, which she will bite off with the umbilical cord and eat. She will then start licking the puppy so roughly that she may appear really violent, but this is actually good for the puppy, getting the breathing started and stimulating the organs and blood supply too. The afterbirth will probably have come on the end of the cord, but if not, it will follow with a couple of hard pushes on the part of the bitch, when she will consume it. You must let her do this, as it helps her over the next hour or two's fasting.

Very soon, about ten minutes later, the next straining starts and eventually another puppy follows, and so on for four or five puppies. She may then take a longish rest, always very nerve-racking for any breeder. Give her a drink of milk which she will usually accept if handed to her in the bed (she will not want to come out). Then leave her and get yourself a snack, because all is not yet over.

After about half an hour go back and see how she is getting on. Soon she will start straining again, but if she goes on resting for much more than an hour, or if she is straining hard and nothing comes and you are sure there are still more puppies unborn, then call your vet. He must come as soon as possible in these cases, before the bitch gets too exhausted.

Once all the puppies are born, see they are settled in a close row, along the milk-bar, and that the bitch is curled round and licking them lazily. Give her another drink of milk (with some sugar added), and then leave her to rest. If she does not settle, then either there are more puppies, or she needs veterinary attention.

Next day I like to get the vet to see the bitch and to give her an injection if he feels that there may still be an afterbirth. The vet knows exactly what to do. Once all is well, change the dirty, scrunched-up newspapers and look at all the pups to see that there are no deformities and not too much white (although a white spot on the chest is allowed, and many of us breeders actually *like* white hollows to the heels).

If there are too many puppies (over seven), you should ask your vet to dispose of some, and then give the bitch a very light meal and again let her rest. She now goes on to at least three snacks a day, and a bigger one for supper, but at first the food must be light, i.e. brown bread, soaked biscuit, fish, with a little chicken or rabbit, but *not* red meat for the first three or four days. Then get her on to ordinary food again.

All should go well, though it is quite usual to lose an odd puppy, damaged inwardly at birth. If all goes well, let her rest quietly, enjoying her puppies for the next couple of weeks, giving her more and better food until she gets on to two good meals a day, morning and night, with a drink of milk or a little snack every time you go to look at the puppies, which should be very frequently at first.

There may be a bit of a crisis at four or five days when she may feel ill and go off her food, or may start to lose her puppies. This could be milk-fever so the vet should come at once. The danger is usually over by about the sixth day.

The puppies' eyes will open on the eleventh day and they will almost immediately start getting on to their legs. On about the eighteenth day they need a first meal of baby cereal and milk, when you may have to teach them to lap by pushing their noses into the dish. If they still will not lap, put a little on your fingers. They will start to suck and after a few sucks will lick your fingers. Once they know about licking, they will start to lap and the first battle is over.

Next day crumble a little brown bread into the cereal and milk and go through it carefully with your fingers to see there are no lumps. On about the twenty-first day you can begin to scrape in a little raw, lean beef just to colour the cereal pinkish, but watch carefully for lumps. By the twenty-fourth day the puppies should be eagerly licking up bread and milk, cereal with the scraped beef, and perhaps a lightly coddled egg.

Once the puppies are feeding well, there is no further difficulty and you get them gradually on to four meals a day using a fine puppy meal as well as brown bread, and they are virtually self-supporting. When they are four weeks old the bitch can leave them all day and go in just for the night. By five weeks she can leave them altogether. At that time they should be wormed for roundworms and their nails cut. At eight weeks they should go to their new homes.

Do not forget your K.C. application form. It should be sent to the Kennel Club with a fee when the pups are approximately two weeks old. In return you will get a 'Breeders Pack' containing a registration form for each pup. You can either register them all yourself or give a registration form duly filled in and signed to the buyer.

You then either clean up completely and disinfect everything and breathe a sigh of relief, or you continue with the one or two puppies you have kept.

Now we are back to the stage where I told you how to rear a puppy, only this time it is one of your own breeding.

Health

I am not a veterinary surgeon, so I am not able to deal with the treatment of diseases. My first advice in this section is to say and indeed to repeat over and over again, 'Tell your vet'. On the other hand, there are various small accidents and other matters, such as cleaning the ears, hardening a sore pad and dealing with minor cuts and bruises, that you can easily deal with yourself, provided that various standard remedies are kept on hand.

For this purpose you need a separate cupboard or small medicine chest, so that there is no possibility of using the dogs' remedies and cotton wool, etc., in a case of human accidents.

I always keep at hand the following:

A supply of cotton bandages of varying widths.

A bottle of mild disinfectant for cuts and a bottle of strong disinfectant for washing kennel floors and scrubbing tables after illness or whelping.

Lint, cotton wool, and a roll of adhesive tape.

A tin of ready-made adhesive dressings of various sizes.

A blunt-ended pair of surgical scissors.

Skin ointment, eye ointment, canker powder.

A good insecticide.

A small bottle of Friars Balsam.

A couple of packets of roundworm tablets and also of tapeworm tablets.

An old toothbrush which has various uses, but is used chiefly as the 'lever' of a tourniquet.

The most important thing is to look at your dog carefully every day and note if its looks and behaviour are absolutely normal. Most dogs seem to feel well all the time, and being creatures of habit, positively ask for their morning run, their titbit, or whatever they have each day. If one morning your dog is reluctant to go out, flags when it is out, refuses food or has a different expression on its face, slightly woe-begone, or a different smell, or if its eyes are runny or mattery, its ear hangs down on one side or the dog squeals when it gets up, sits down, or when you touch it, then you may be in for a bit of trouble and must take immediate steps.

If you think a vet should see the dog, I strongly advise that. If it is something you cannot see an immediate cause for, then *call your vet* and do it at once before the dog gets really ill.

Many bad illnesses can be nipped in the bud if the vet gets there at the first sign of trouble. But at the same time, do not fuss. If you can see that the cause of the lameness is a slightly cracked pad, then you can deal with that. Also you can cope if it hangs its ear or shows signs of worms.

But running eyes, a badly upset tummy, a temperature, fever, or a cough, are all possible signs of something rather more serious, and that is when you should immediately get on that phone to the vet's surgery. Do not wait to find out if the green mattery eyes are distemper. Get it stopped at once and in time, by calling early for your vet.

Although I may not prescribe for the various illnesses, I can at least warn you of the symptoms, so that you can watch out for them, thus being prepared.

Mattery or runny eyes have various causes and need vet's treatment and advice. If the eyes have a green or yellow mattery discharge, that can mean distemper, a dreaded disease. Call the vet immediately whether your dog is inoculated against the disease or not. The immunisation can occasionally break down.

If the discharge is a big pearl-white drop at the corners and the whites of the eye are shell-pink under the upper eyelid, then this may be kennel cough, a mild disease itself, but leading to dangerous after-effects. So again, the vet must be called as soon as possible. Try and remember if you heard the dog husk in its throat or nasal passages, as though it was trying to clear a small fish bone or piece of straw. If so tell your vet. It may have happened quite a few days ago, or even a couple of weeks. The vet will decide whether the dog has kennel cough or distemper, or if it is just a harmless cold, which some, though not many, dogs are subject to. Treat this white pearl-drop and the shell-pink whites in the upper eye as serious until you hear the vet tell you it isn't.

In all these cases the dog will run a temperature, high in distemper, about 103-105°F (39.5°C-40.4°C); only about 102½-103½°F (39°C-39.75°C) in kennel cough and then very intermittent and fluctuating; and only about 102-102½°F (39°C) in a common cold and that for only a day, or at the most two days. The normal temperature of a dog is 101½°F (38.5°C) in an adult, and 102-102½°F (39°C) in a puppy up to about six months.

Watery eyes may be a cold (see above) or it may be a sign of a hereditary disease called entropion.

Entropion is caused by the eyelid rolling in on itself towards the eyeball. The hairs of the skin and eyelashes are then directly against the delicate membrane on the eye itself. This needs veterinary attention and possibly a small operation to correct the rolling in of the skin and eyelashes surrounding the eye. It may occur in one eye or in both. Only a vet can help this trouble. I myself do not breed from an affected dog or bitch because of the hereditary factor.

There is one more possible cause of watery eyes and that is dirty ears, there being a connection between the eye and the ear.

Dirty ears can be dealt with yourself if you keep watch early in the puppy's life and attend regularly to them, as I have told you in the section on grooming. Keep a good preparation of canker powder (because dirty ears are usually caused by canker, a mite that irritates the lining of the ears causing liquid to collect if left untreated). I use an old remedy of 1 part boracic powder, ½ part zinc oxide, and ¼ part iodoform. I get this made up at an old-fashioned chemist and keep it in a jar with a tightly screwed top. It *must* be kept absolutely airtight and in either a dark-glassed jar or in the dark of a cupboard. This remedy is now difficult to get, but there are plenty of good preparations which your pet shop will sell you for this purpose. I prefer my old well-tried recipe and never have ear trouble in my Labradors. If you see your dog hanging an ear, then urgent treatment is needed.

Never neglect canker, as it leads to many other troubles, such as shaking the ears frequently, when they themselves can become filled with liquid or blood and thus may need a rather serious and unsightly operation to release the fluid. So always keep a bottle of canker powder in your medicine chest and watch the ears carefully for a reddish-brown dirt inside, a musty smell, persistent head-shaking or a hanging ear. Use your remedy, seeing that it gets well down into the bottom of the ear. If you do let canker become bad so that the ear channels swell and fill up, then veterinary attention is needed, but this means that you have neglected the matter yourself, to let it get so bad.

Do not push about inside the ear with an orange stick covered with cotton wool. The ear is very delicate and if you have got to the stage where you have to use this, then let the vet do it. He knows how.

Sore feet are caused by various things. First there are cuts, which usually cannot be stitched, so if they are bad, the dog will need a vet. For a very slight cut wash with a *very* mild disinfectant, then bandage tightly right round the whole foot or leg. *Do not fasten with a safety pin.* Use a strip or two of the adhesive roll from your medicine chest, or split the bandage-end so that you can tie a knot, but *no pins.* Dogs love to eat them. About twenty minutes later, loosen the bandage and re-bandage less tightly if the bleeding has completely stopped. The second cause of sore feet is cracked pads. For this pour a little *undiluted* Friars Balsam into a shallow dish. Dip the sole of the foot into it and hold it in for a few minutes. The dog may dislike it at first as it may sting, but hold it in firmly, then hold the foot up in the air and blow on it till the Friars Balsam dries completely. Repeat this for a couple of days and the soreness will go out of the pads and they will harden up. Try to keep the solution off the dog's hair or it will become sticky.

The third cause of sore feet is a swelling or hot lump which causes great pain. This is very common in dogs and is called interdigital cyst, coming up between the toes. Treat exactly as above with the Friars Balsam. Interdigital cysts in Labradors are usually due to a slight loss of condition, so the dog should be toned up with a tonic such as vitamin B in the form of yeast, or by a dash of apple cider vinegar on the daily food which is a great tonic for any form of debility or run-down condition. A day or two's application of Friars Balsam should stop them successfully, but they may recur. If they continue to be painful after a course of the Balsam treatment, tell your vet. The cysts may need lancing or cutting out, but they are usually very responsive to the treatment and I have never had to call the vet to operate on a dog. Keep your kennel floor very dry, as damp can cause the cysts, as can wet autumn leaves and sour ground.

The treatment for cuts depends on the severity. If the cut is a bad one and is streaming or, worse still, pulsing blood out, then get someone to hold the dog's leg tightly above the wound to try and control the bleeding. Meanwhile do not panic but go quickly to your medicine chest and get out a suitable bandage and the old toothbrush, or if this is not available a pen or pencil. Bandage *above* the wound and then insert the

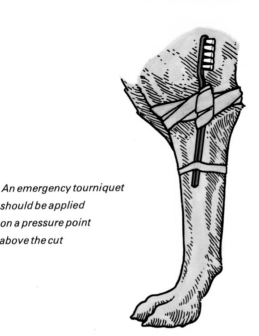

*An emergency tourniquet
should be applied
on a pressure point
above the cut*

toothbrush handle or pen or pencil. Turn very tightly and then bandage the ends into the tight position, thus making a tourniquet.

Then bandage the actual wound also tightly, but without disinfecting. Then let your assistant hold the leg and see the toothbrush keeps in place. If you have no assistant, take the dog with you as best you can and get to the telephone and call the vet. This is an emergency and if your own vet is unavailable then call another firm of vets, or even a doctor. The tourniquet must be released every ten minutes for a few moments, to restore the blood-flow to the limb, otherwise damage may result; but as soon as you can, restore the tourniquet. Keep doing this until professional help arrives.

Bruises do not really concern Labradors because the coat is so thick it takes some force to get through it; but if your dog is hit by a car, call the vet to see there is no internal or bone damage. Once he says all is well, and that it is just a bad bruise, then you need not really do much about it except make the dog a comfortable bed and let it rest if it wants, and keep it warm till

A bitch may need to have an improvised muzzle when being mated

it recovers from the shock. The bruise will heal itself in very little time.

Sprains, strains, and broken bones all need a vet's advice or treatment. Your dog will need a plaster cast in most cases of breaks, and lesser strains or sprains may need infra-red lamp treatment, which *must* be done under veterinary supervision and advice, or internal burns and over-radiation may very likely occur.

Scratching and niggling at the skin or fur usually means the dog has picked up either fleas or small lice. Use your insect powder as bought from your pet shop. If the biting persists, ask your vet because it could be harvest mites or mange mites, which burrow under the skin so are not reached by surface application of flea powder.

If the dog bites at the root of his tail, rubs on the ground or gets wet, red, raw patches round the base of its tail, then it is either eczema, a blocked anal gland or worms. If the dog has been kept regularly wormed as it should be, then it is not likely to be worms, so suspect anal gland trouble or eczema. Your

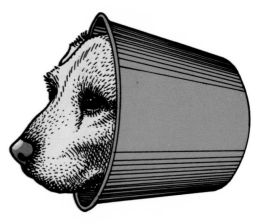

A plastic bucket adapted to prevent a dog from irritating a wound

vet will squeeze the anal gland for you or you can do it yourself if properly taught by a vet. If it is diagnosed as eczema, a non-infectious skin trouble, the cause will be wrong feeding, and what we call over-heated blood. (The blood does not actually get too hot. This is a term meaning that the body is having too rich a diet for the sort and size and exercise of dog or from too hot weather.) The dog cannot sweat except through the mouth, so the body cannot get rid of impurities and the rich diet upsets the metabolism.

Feeding with boiled green foods, such as nettles, or cabbage leaves or cauliflower leaves, helps to keep the blood 'cool' or, rather, helps the metabolism. The addition of a little flowers of sulphur to the food also helps, but usually a change of diet with much less meat and rich food is indicated. Such foods as maize, as fed to cattle in flakes, is very 'heating', as is also too rich biscuit. A Labrador does better on a much less rich diet. Use a plain biscuit meal, plenty of greens well boiled, and the biscuit soaked in the vegetable water. Let the dog eat grass if it wants. Cut down the food, especially sugary biscuits and give only one part meat to three parts biscuit. This helps to keep the skin clean and healthy.

Harvest mites and all forms of mange need urgent vet's treatment.

Digestive upsets may be caused by too rich food, tainted food, or the dog may have eaten some filth that disagrees with it. *Stiffen* the diet, removing all milk, liver and rich food. Give a

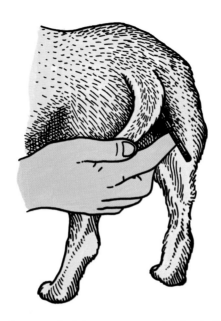

The normal adult temperature of a dog is 101.5°F

Applying ointment to the eye

small stiff meal with boiled rice in it. Do not feed slops or put the dog on to a milk diet. These are laxatives. Cut out all fat, too.

If there is blood in the runny motion, call the vet because this is either gastritis or a bone pricking the intestine, and may be serious. If the loose motions persist, your vet will give you a bottle of medicine to help. Usually digestive upsets are better by next day but if not, call the vet.

I think I have given the most usual small ailments that affect a pet dog or even a shooting dog in his everyday life.

Now we come to the three hereditary diseases of the Labrador. The first is progressive retinal atrophy (PRA), a condition that causes actual blindness in the dog at about three or four years old, but which can be spotted by an expert in the disease at eighteen months or even sooner. Any dog may inherit this if it has certain bloodlines in its pedigree. Reputable breeders have *all* their breeding stock checked by one of the official scrutineers, often at a veterinary college, and sessions are also held at the various club rallies up and down the country so that people get a chance to have their dog's eyes tested. We breeders do this with every dog. If the dog is clear of the disease at eighteen months, the scrutineer gives both you and the Kennel Club an Interim Certificate of Clearness from PRA. The dog is tested again at the age of four and if it is still clear gets a Permanent Certificate and need never be done again. But if either of these examinations shows that the dog is affected, then it is the wisest and indeed only course to have it put down by a vet, because it will certainly go blind, a tragic and pathetic end to it. This is by far the worst of the three hereditary diseases, but luckily is now very rare in Labradors.

The second disease is hip (or shoulder) dysplasia (HD). This is a nuisance only if the dog is lame. If you are a breeder, then you must come to terms with this disease and formulate your own policy, because you are sure to breed a few puppies which eventually prove to have it. It seems to be an occupational hazard of the breed and no attempts have yet succeeded in breeding it out.

It will appear in two ways. Either the dog will be stiff in getting up, or lame usually in a back leg, but sometimes in a shoulder. If you are a breeder or a shooting man, this is a nuisance and the dog should be given away to a good home, telling the owners, of course, what is wrong; but if the disease is too bad the dog should, for kindness sake, be put down.

If, however, it is not too bad and the dog can manage very well, then if it is your pet, why put it down? You need not breed from it, but it can lead a perfectly happy, healthy, pet life. There may be a touch of rheumatism when it gets older but that happens anyway in most cases of old dogs and you need not destroy the dog for it. Just see that the dog has some comforts such as a good drying when it is wet and a comfortable bed.

Sometimes hip dysplasia does not show at all in the dog. Someone tells you that you must have your dog X-rayed, and you find surprisingly that it has HD. Then most certainly do not fuss and put the dog down if it is perfectly sound and free from pain. Many good shooting dogs have a touch of HD and so do many pets and indeed show or field trial dogs. It often shows only on an X-ray, not in their daily lives and outwardly they are perfectly normal. Most Labradors will remain strong and you will never know they have it. So long as the dog is sound and free from lameness, then do not bother to incur the expense of an X-ray. If you are going to breed from your Labrador then that is different. I am writing primarily for pet owners.

The third disease is entropion, which I have already dealt with. The affected dog should *not* be bred from, but a small operation will put the condition right so that the dog can lead a comfortable life.

It is very rare to find a Labrador that does not love water

The breed worldwide

Although the Labrador was originally found in Newfoundland, spreading with the fishing boats to Poole Harbour and thence to the shooting men of Britain, funnily enough it is from Britain that it has spread all over the world. At first it had a struggle to obtain a footing against the traditional dogs of those countries that imported it, but gradually the many virtues of the breed were recognised and now the Labrador is known in virtually every country in the world, from the most northerly point of Canada where teams of Labradors have sometimes won the sledging races over snow against all the traditional Husky breeds, to New Zealand where the showing cult is rapidly taking hold, and the Labrador is becoming more and more popular.

This is the general history of the breed overseas, but I would like to elaborate on the chief countries that have adopted it, have adapted it to their own needs and are now as keen as we are in Britain.

America has for many years been a stronghold of Labradors, both in the show ring and in field trials. At the time of writing, blacks are still very much to the fore although many English yellows are now being imported so that some of the big kennels now have as many yellows as blacks, which may in the very near future change the balance of the colours. But at the moment there are good blacks a-plenty, outshining the yellows. The Americans go especially for spectacular black males, importing more dogs from Britain, and lately from Sweden, than bitches.

I have had quite a bit to do with the American Labrador breeders, many of whom I am proud to count as close friends and, as a general rule, I would think of them more as avidly keen competitors both in the show ring and the field than as dedicated breeders. The reason is two-fold. Firstly that for some reason in nearly every country in the world there is an in-built difficulty in keeping up the quality of the home-bred stock for more than two or at the most three generations, possibly because of the very hot sunshine and lack of rain, which tends to draw the puppies 'up' instead of 'out'. Thus in a few generations very tall, slim, leggy Labradors are produced, not at all what is wanted in the breed. The second reason is that Americans set far more store on their show wins than do the

British, liking the spectacular, very handsome, showy dog, while we in Britain prefer our less spectacular, more 'typy', and unexaggerated medium-sized bitches, the sort to breed from. In the long run the strength of any kennel lies in its bitches, which has been said a thousand times but seems only to be fully understood in Great Britain and Ireland. There is another good reason why the Americans are keener on the actual win than the British are. In the USA they are not allowed to show their champions in any class other than the special class provided. So the championship points always go to a Labrador that is not a champion. This means that every dog is in with a chance for those points without having to beat any established champions. This makes for extreme keenness and expectancy of success, but also to a far lower standard of champions, because in Britain one has to beat the very best to get one's champion title, while in America they only have to beat the best of the non-champions. Thus they have a great incentive to win, making a new champion every four or five shows. Then, if the Labrador is not a good champion able to take on all the rest of the good ones in the Specials class it can sink into oblivion, while a new champion arises in the same kennel.

In spite of this generality of making cheap champions, there are always a few kennels in America as in Britain which are outstanding for the quality of their stock, able to win many Groups and Specials classes and therefore known and respected throughout the world. Most of the present day winning stock contains the very best of the British bloodlines, which have been used with great success on the American bred Labradors.

A great name in American Labradors, not depending on imported stock, but producing Dual Champion after Dual Champion, was Ardens. I never saw one in the flesh but the many photographs of these great dogs, such as Dual Ch. Shed of Arden, show them to be outstanding. How I wish that we could have used some of that successful dual purpose stock over here in Britain.

Sweden is another great country for Labradors, having started with untypical Labradors just for work, and then suddenly realised they were on the wrong lines, doing a great deal of research in a very thorough manner and then importing splendid British breeding lines. In a very few generations they were breeding very good typical stock, as they do to this day

They still import a great deal, keeping their bloodlines fluid and using British stock to the best advantage. They are very clever and thorough students of bloodlines and are progressing by leaps and bounds.

Swedish influence is now spreading to Norway, where very good Labradors are becoming more and more popular, some excellent shows being held there. The Swedish stock is allowed to travel to Norway for shows and trials and *vice versa,* which makes each of these sister countries keep their socks pulled up in order to take on the others.

A wonderful thing about the Norwegian breeders (and this applies to the Swedes too), is that they are prepared to fly their dogs enormous distances to use the *right* dog for their bitch, not having a parochial dog-next-door attitude, and this makes for fluid bloodlines and a very high standard of home-bred stock.

While I was judging in Sweden, a Finnish bitch was there being mated to a Swedish dog and this sets the pattern of the Swedes, the Finns, and the Norwegians as breeders, as well as excellent exhibitors both in shows and trials.

Again there are some 'Master' kennels which set the pace and keep the standard high. These are the ones that provide the good stud dogs and breed the good bitches. They also import the best that they can buy in Britain, being regular visitors to British shows and trials, thus keeping their fingers on the pulse and seeing how they can import to improve their home-bred stock.

Another stronghold of the Labradors is Australia, and New Zealand to a lesser degree, because they are only just starting to be extremely keen, importing both from Australia and Britain. Tremendous shows are held in Australia, exhibitors travelling huge distances to reach them. The Sydney Royal goes on for about eight days I believe, the Labrador classes being a great event often with a famous overseas judge from Britain to judge them. The basic bloodlines of the Australian Labradors are British, thus also the New Zealand section of the breed. The Australians are keen breeders importing very many good stud dogs from Britain and the USA, but here is a country that has the difficulty of their Labradors being drawn 'up on the leg' by the sun and therefore new, shorter legged blood is needed every few generations. I do not think New Zealand will have quite the same difficulty, because their climate is rather more like the British climate, a bit softer and damper.

I have one small 'but' about most of the aforementioned countries and that is that they import more and better dogs than they do bitches, which means they are using very excellent dogs on bitches that may be slightly mediocre or perhaps may be third generation home-bred, when the sun has had its leggy effect on them. This does not really give these good imported males the best of chances to improve the Standard, and I feel when talking to their Labrador people or judging their Labradors that this is one reason for having continually to import to keep their own stock up to standard.

Not so in Kenya, Rhodesia and South Africa, three countries becoming very keen indeed, especially on showing. Their trials are well supported but in the two last-mentioned countries seem to take rather a second place.

Funnily enough, the climate of Kenya seems to suit the Labrador and some excellent stock is bred there. Equal attention in Kenya is given to the working and show side, which makes for a splendid dual purpose dog. The stock seems to breed pretty true, but in spite of this there are not enough Labradors to make the breed self-supporting, so frequent imports are necessary. Equal emphasis is given to a good bitch and good dog, both being imported so that the standard remains at a very good level, with overseas bloodlines setting the standard. There is one unfortunate thing which is that, although the dogs look extremely well and live very happily indeed, having a truly lovely life, with plenty of work and excitement, Africa is well-known for its hazards to man and beast of fevers, rather dangerous working conditions and the occasional leopard, so that accidents and illnesses happen rather more frequently than in Britain. The Kenyan breeders therefore have the heartbreak of losing some of their beautiful young stock. This means yet once again that they are dependent on good bloodlines from overseas, not only to fill the gaps, but to add much needed fresh blood to the rather small nucleus of Labradors in Kenya; but the Kenyans undoubtedly make the very best of what they have got.

South Africa and Rhodesia do not suffer quite the same hazards to the same extent, but again they have imported some lovely stock from Britain and have a great eye for a good bitch, importing good females from Britain wherever they can find them. They are a nation of breeders as well as exhibitors, and also run trials, though not to the same extent as the Kenyans do, the opportunities for work being rather less than in Kenya. But like the Kenyans they have some excellent stock and breed some good puppies too. The chief reason for their imports is to keep the bloodlines from becoming clogged with too much line or inbreeding, thus needing some fresh blood from time to time. They do suffer a little from the home-bred stock going 'up on the leg' but again not as quickly as in Australia. But in all three African countries I saw good, typical Labradors, both home-bred and imported.

I have not mentioned the tremendously good dogs in Ireland, both north and south, having counted these in with the good British stock which is second to none. The Irish are famous as breeders of livestock of all kinds and their Labradors are no exception, so they differ in no way from those in England, Wales and Scotland. The same lines are used most cleverly, their good dogs are the tops both for show and work, they come over and take on all the British good dogs and often beat them, even in such shows as Crufts.

So I will not go on about Ireland other than to say again that they are so intermingled with British bloodlines as to be able to breed as good stock as British breeders, and to beat British dogs with their best both at shows and trials. Indeed many countries are using the Irish bloodlines and exports to their great advantage.

Many other countries such as France, Holland, and Belgium are well established and are breeding very good stock and getting more numerous and better quality Labradors all the time. Italy, Hungary and Czechoslovakia are just starting to recognise the excellence of the breed, especially for work. They are starting to import high class British stock and we shall see these countries becoming keen on the Labrador just as in the case of the principal Labrador breeding countries specifically mentioned in this chapter.

Labrador bloodlines

The first kennels of Labradors in this country were the Buccleuchs, the Netherbys and those of the Earl of Home.

From the Buccleuchs, mated to dogs owned by those other sporting gentlemen, descend all the black Labradors of today, the common ancestor to all blacks being Buccleuch Avon who lived around the late 1880s. From these descended the Mundens, the Whitmores, and from them the great Banchory Labradors, the most famous of all time owned by the Rt. Hon. Lorna Countess Howe, whose name is immortal wherever the Labrador is known. The first registered yellow, around the beginning of the century, was Ben of Hyde, his blood being developed by a handful of breeders such as Col. Radclyffe, whose descendant Mrs. Audrey Radclyffe is still breeding yellow Labradors today. The Macphersons in Scotland bred them almost from the start and the doyenne of all yellow breeders, Mrs. Wormald, is still with us, with her own Knaith strain still going strong although she is now well over ninety. She still has some very handsome dogs, descendants of her old Mannie, who was a son of Ben of Hyde. So Mrs. Wormald has been breeding the same strain for over sixty years. She is a great lady and I count myself lucky to have known and been very much helped by both these two great ladies in Labradors, Lorna Countess Howe and Mrs. Arthur Wormald, who incidentally, in spite of her great age, is Secretary of the Yellow Labrador Club and has her fingers very much on the reins.

The Banchorys went on winning both at shows and in trials until the decade after the Second World War, but a new kennel started before the war was now building up and when with the death of Lady Howe the Banchorys were no more, our present leader in Labradors took over the premier position which she still holds today. These are the world-famous Sandylands Kennels which are the greatest influence in the world at present, and are owned by Mrs. Gwen Broadley.

These famous names in Labradors from 1885 until the present day are the strains that practically every Labrador in the world descends from today and I shall be very surprised if, when you get interested enough to trace your Labrador's pedigree right back to its beginning, it does not come down from the kennels named.

Most of the names are now out of the back of the present day pedigrees but you will almost certainly find a strong Sandylands influence close behind your own puppy. There will also almost certainly be some Poppletons, a famous Second World War kennel, started just prior to the outbreak but only blossoming into great power in the immediate post-war years. The Poppletons too are now gone, but happily the Sandyland Labradors are as strong as ever and still easily the leading kennel of Labradors in the world.

Other good names you may find and be proud of in your pedigree are the Poolstead kennels, Ballyduff, Nokeener, Zelstone, Knaith, Blaircourt, Timspring, Follytower, Landyke, Heatheredge, Mansergh, Diant, Cornlands, Liddly and Lawnwood and indeed many more good kennels such as Wendover, Cookridge, Whatstandwell and Kinley. Although one or two of these strains are now finished or in abeyance, most of them are still going from strength to strength and indeed are the leading kennels of today.

Most of these kennels breed all colours, although the Knaiths have always been yellow only and the Manserghs black only. Cookridge have lately largely specialised in chocolates, almost to the exclusion of other colours, although a few blacks are still kept to help the chocolate keep its true deep shade. See many of these names in your pedigree and you will know you are on good, well-bred bloodlines and that they will be recognised and respected by Labrador breeders all over the world.

READING LIST

Kinsella, Miriam. *Labradors.* Arthur Barker Ltd., 1972.

Roslin-Williams, Mary. *The Dual Purpose Labrador.* Pelham Books Ltd., 1969.

Roslin-Williams, Mary. *All About the Labrador.* Pelham Books Ltd., 1975.

Warwick, Helen. *The Complete Labrador Retriever.* Howell Book House, USA.

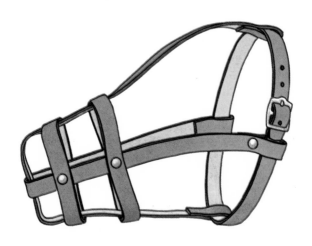

A suitable muzzle for use when required or advised

USEFUL ADDRESSES

The Kennel Club, 1 Clarges Street, Piccadilly, London W1Y 8AB, England.

The American Kennel Club, 51 Madison Avenue, New York, N.Y. 10010, U.S.A.

There are many clubs catering for this breed and the addresses of these can be obtained from your Kennel Club.

DOG MAGAZINES

Pure Bred Dogs, the American Kennel Gazette, published by the American Kennel Club.

Dog World, 22 New Street, Ashford, Kent, England.

Our Dogs, 5 Oxford Road Station Approach, Manchester 1, England.

Index